GAO

Report to the Chairman, Committee on Finance, U.S. Senate

I0469276

December 2012

HIGHER EDUCATION

A Small Percentage of Families Save in 529 Plans

GAO

Accountability ★ Integrity ★ Reliability

GAO-13-64

December 2012

HIGHER EDUCATION

A Small Percentage of Families Save in 529 Plans

Why GAO Did This Study

Paying for college is becoming more challenging, partly because of rising tuition rates. A college savings plan can be an option to help meet these costs. To encourage families to save for college, earnings from 529 plans—named after section 529 of the Internal Revenue Code—grow tax-deferred and are exempt from federal income tax when they are used for qualified higher education expenses. In fiscal year 2011, the Department of the Treasury estimated these plans represented $1.6 billion in forgone federal revenue. Managed by states, over one hundred 529 plan options were available to families nationwide as of July 2012. The number of 529 plan accounts and the amount invested in them has grown during the past decade. GAO was asked to describe (1) the percentage and characteristics of families enrolling in 529 plans, (2) plan features and other factors that affect participation in 529 plans, and (3) the extent to which savings in 529 plans affect financial aid awards. GAO analyzed government data, including the SCF. This survey's 529 plan data are combined with Coverdells, so the SCF estimates used in the report include both 529 and Coverdell data. GAO also analyzed National Postsecondary Student Aid Study data; conducted interviews with federal and state officials, industry and academic experts, and state and institutional higher education officials; reviewed 529 plan and Department of Education documents; conducted a literature review; and reviewed relevant federal laws, regulations, and guidance.

What GAO Recommends

GAO is not making any recommendations in this report.

View GAO-13-64. For more information, contact Michelle Sager, (202) 512-6806, sagerm@gao.gov

What GAO Found

A small percentage of U.S. families saved in 529 plans in 2010, and those who did tended to be wealthier than others. According to the Survey of Consumer Finances (SCF), less than 3 percent of families saved in a 529 plan or Coverdell Education Savings Account (Coverdell)—a similar but less often used college savings vehicle also included in the SCF. While the economic downturn may have reduced income available for education savings, even among those families who considered saving for education a priority, fewer than 1 in 10 had a 529 plan (or Coverdell). Families with these accounts had about 25 times the median financial assets of those without. They also had about 3 times the median income and the percentage who had college degrees was about twice as high as for families without 529 plans (or Coverdells).

States offer consumers a variety of 529 plan features that, along with several other factors, can affect participation. Some of the most important features families consider when choosing a 529 plan are tax benefits, fees, and investment options, according to experts and state officials GAO interviewed. These features can vary across the state plans. For example, in July 2012, total annual asset-based fees ranged from 0 to 2.78 percent depending on the type of plan. 529 plan officials and experts GAO interviewed said participation is also affected by families' ability to save, their awareness of 529 plans as a savings option, and the difficulty in choosing a plan given the amount of variation between plans (see fig. 1). Selected states, however, have taken steps to address these barriers. For example, to address families' ability to save, particularly for low-income families, some states have adopted plans that include less risky investments, have low minimum contributions, and match families' contributions.

Factors that Affect 529 Plan Participation

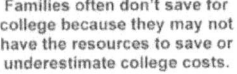

| Families often don't save for college because they may not have the resources to save or underestimate college costs. | For families who do save, many don't know how a 529 plan could help them. | Even families who want to take advantage of a 529 plan can have trouble selecting and using one. |

Source: GAO analysis based on reports and interviews with 529 plan officials and experts.

Savings in 529 plans affect financial aid similarly to a family's other assets. For federal aid, a family's assets affect how much it is expected to contribute to the cost of college. If the amount of those assets exceeds a certain threshold, then a percentage is expected to be used for college costs. For example, for students who are dependent on their parents, the percentage of parental assets, including savings in 529 plans, that the family may be expected to contribute ranges from 2.64 to 5.64 percent. Many states and selected institutions also treat 529 plan savings the same as other family assets. However, a few states provide them with special treatment, such as exempting those funds from their financial aid calculation.

_____ **United States Government Accountability Office**

Contents

Abbreviations

Coverdells	Coverdell Education Savings Accounts
CSPN	College Savings Plan Network
Education	Department of Education
EFC	expected family contribution
EGTRRA	Economic Growth and Tax Relief Reconciliation Act of 2001
FAFSA	Free Application for Federal Student Aid
FDIC	Federal Deposit Insurance Corporation
Federal Reserve	Board of Governors of the Federal Reserve System
IRS	Internal Revenue Service
MSRB	Municipal Securities Rulemaking Board
NBER	National Bureau of Economic Research
NPSAS	National Postsecondary Student Aid Study
SEC	Securities and Exchange Commission
SCF	Survey of Consumer Finances
SOI	Statistics of Income
Treasury	Department of the Treasury

United States Government Accountability Office
Washington, DC 20548

December 12, 2012

The Honorable Max Baucus
Chairman
Committee on Finance
United States Senate

Dear Mr. Chairman:

While median family income decreased between 2005 and 2011, college tuition and fees increased at an average annual rate of 6 percent, more than double the rate of inflation. As families look for ways to prepare for these rising costs, their options include saving in advance; paying for expenses at the time they occur out-of-pocket and/or through grants and scholarships; or financing the cost through educational loans that they repay at a later date. Loans have become an increasingly popular option to cover these costs.[1] However, with college loan balances now estimated at $914 billion, more than total credit card debt,[2] financing a large portion of college costs potentially creates a future financial burden for students and their families. To encourage people to save for college expenses in advance, Congress, in 1996, added section 529 to the Internal Revenue Code, which authorized state qualified tuition programs, otherwise known as 529 plans.[3] These plans are available in two forms— prepaid tuition plans and college savings plans. In prepaid tuition plans, participants buy tuition credits or certificates on behalf of a designated

---

[1] The College Board reported that the relative stability of the ratio of grant to loan amounts over time indicates that loans have not replaced grants. However, grant aid often fails to increase rapidly enough to fill the growing gap between the costs of attending college and the ability of students and families to pay those costs. College Board Advocacy and Policy Center, *Trends in Student Aid 2011* (New York, NY: 2011).

[2] Federal Reserve Bank of New York, Research and Statistics Group, Microeconomic Studies. *Quarterly Report on Household Debt and Credit.* (New York, NY: August 2012). Debt amount is as of second quarter 2012.

[3] Small Business Job Protection Act of 1996, Pub. L. No. 104 -188 § 1806, 110 Stat. 1755, 1895, codified at 26 U.S.C. § 529.

　　　　　　　　　　　　　　　　　　　　　　　　GAO-13-64 529 Plans

beneficiary, who can use them for qualified higher education expenses.[4] College savings plans allow for contributions to an account for the purpose of paying a designated beneficiary's qualified higher education expenses. As of July 2012, more than one hundred 529 plan options have been developed and are managed by states and the District of Columbia. In 2011, there were more than 11 million accounts with assets of $167 billion (in 2012 dollars).[5]

While there is no federal tax deduction for payments or contributions to 529 plans, which are made with after-tax dollars, plan earnings accumulate tax-deferred and earnings included in withdrawals used to pay for qualified higher education expenses are not taxed. This tax expenditure cost the federal government an estimated $1.6 billion in forgone revenue in fiscal year 2011.[6] We reported, in 2012, that higher income households are more likely to have 529 plans and tend to benefit more from these tax preferences because of their higher marginal tax

---

[4] Qualified higher education expenses include tuition, books, supplies, and equipment. Costs for room and board are considered qualified education expenses if students are enrolled at least half-time. Qualified higher education expenses also included expenses paid or incurred in 2009 and 2010 for computer technology, equipment, or Internet access and related services. Eligible educational institutions include colleges, universities, vocational schools, or other postsecondary institutions eligible to participate in a federal student aid program authorized by Title IV of the Higher Education Act of 1965, as amended. This includes virtually all accredited, public, nonprofit, and for-profit postsecondary institutions in the U.S.

[5] Data provided by the Financial Research Corporation. Account numbers and assets are as of year-end 2011.

[6] Tax expenditures are reductions in a federal taxpayer's tax liability that result from special credits, deductions, exemptions and exclusions, deferrals of tax liability, and preferential tax rates. The federal revenue forgone may be viewed as spending channeled through the tax code. This estimate by the Department of the Treasury (Treasury) includes both college savings plans and prepaid plans. For fiscal year 2011, the Joint Committee on Taxation reported revenue loss estimates of $500 million for college savings plans and less than $50 million for prepaid plans. Revenue loss estimates do not incorporate any behavioral responses and, thus, do not necessarily represent the exact amount of revenue that would be gained if a specific tax expenditure was repealed.

rate.[7] We have recommended in the past that tax expenditures be periodically reviewed to determine their effectiveness in achieving specific policy goals, particularly given the nation's long-term fiscal imbalance.[8]

In response to your request to examine the extent to which 529 plans help families of all income levels save for college and how these plans affect student financial aid, we reviewed (1) the percentage and characteristics of families enrolling in 529 plans, (2) the plan features and other factors that affect participation in 529 plans, and (3) the extent to which savings in 529 plans affect financial aid awards.

To answer these research objectives, we analyzed government and industry data; conducted interviews with federal and state officials, industry representatives and academic experts, as well as state and institutional higher education officials; reviewed 529 plan and Department of Education (Education) documents; conducted a literature review; and reviewed relevant federal laws, regulations, and guidance. We assessed the reliability of the data we used by reviewing documentation, interviewing knowledgeable officials, and conducting electronic testing on relevant data fields. We found the data we reviewed reliable for the purposes of our analyses.

To determine the percentage and characteristics of families enrolling in 529 plans, we reviewed data from the 2010 Survey of Consumer Finances (SCF); the 2007-2008 National Postsecondary Student Aid Study (NPSAS), which was the most recent available and which we adjusted to 2010 dollars; and 2007-2010 Statistics of Income (SOI) federal tax data. Our analysis of data from SCF, NPSAS, and SOI are

---

[7] GAO, *Higher Education: Improved Tax Information Could Help Families Pay for College*, GAO-12-560 (Washington, D.C.: May 18, 2012). The analysis used in this report also included Coverdell Education Savings Accounts (Coverdells). Similar to 529 plans, Coverdell accounts allow families to save for education expenses. Account earnings accumulate tax-deferred and earnings included in withdrawals used to pay for qualified education expenses are not subject to federal tax. Unlike 529 plans, (1) Coverdell contributors must generally have a modified adjusted gross income of less than $110,000 per year ($220,000 in the case of a joint return), (2) Coverdells have annual contribution limits of $2,000 that must generally stop when a beneficiary reaches 18 years of age, and (3) Coverdells can be used for qualified elementary, secondary, or postsecondary expenses typically for individuals under age 30.

[8] GAO, *Government Performance and Accountability: Tax Expenditures Represent a Substantial Federal Commitment and Need to Be Reexamined*, GAO-05-690 (Washington, D.C.: Sept. 23, 2005).

subject to sampling errors because these data sets are based on samples. Unless otherwise noted, all percentage estimates based on SCF, NPSAS, and SOI have 95 percent confidence intervals that are within 5 percentage points of the estimate itself, and all numerical estimates other than percentages have 95 percent confidence intervals that are within 5 percent of the estimate itself. Using SCF data, we generated estimates of the characteristics of households—including wealth (financial assets), income, education, and race/ethnicity—enrolled in 529 plans or Coverdell Education Savings Accounts (Coverdells)[9] and compared those to characteristics of families not enrolled in these plans. Our estimates are based on analyses from the restricted SCF dataset and were conducted with assistance from officials at the Board of Governors of the Federal Reserve System (Federal Reserve). We also developed a profile of the general college population using NPSAS data. In addition, we analyzed taxpayer data from SOI and used a microsimulation model from the National Bureau of Economic Research to understand the extent to which taxpayers use withdrawals (known as distributions) from 529 plans for qualified educational expenses and how the tax savings from these plans are distributed across income levels.

To understand the features and factors that affect participation, we interviewed officials from five state 529 plans (Louisiana, Michigan, Pennsylvania, Utah, and Virginia), conducted a literature review, and spoke with academic researchers, industry regulators, financial services companies, financial experts, and consumer interest groups. While we selected the five state plans to represent variety in the types of plans offered, benefits, and geographic location, our findings cannot be generalized to all 529 plans. We also analyzed College Savings Plan Network (CSPN) data to provide a national overview of plan features and benefits.[10] To provide information on the percentage of students who receive financial aid and the median award amount, we analyzed NPSAS data. To assess efforts by states to disclose 529 plan information to consumers, we reviewed disclosure documents from selected states as well as CSPN disclosure principles.

---

[9] The SCF codes responses for 529 plans and Coverdells together. Survey officials said respondents did not always distinguish between the two account types; therefore, we were unable to separate these responses because of data reliability concerns.

[10] CSPN is an affiliate to the National Association of State Treasurers and serves as a clearinghouse for information on 529 plans. Plan data are as of July 2012.

We assessed the extent to which savings in 529 plans affect federal financial aid awards by reviewing relevant federal laws, regulations, and guidance, and interviewing Education officials. In addition, we analyzed NPSAS data to determine the extent to which a family's total assets affected the federal expected family contribution to college expenses. To understand how savings in 529 plans affect state and institutional financial aid, we interviewed six state financial aid offices and six institutions of higher education. We selected states that indicated on a National Association of State Student Grant and Aid Programs survey that they used a financial aid formula other than the federal methodology in their primary needs analysis and/or provided special treatment for state 529 plans. We selected an institution in each of the six states that was reported as using the College Board's PROFILE or another institutional form, in addition to the Free Application for Federal Student Aid, to gather information used in making decisions regarding institutional financial aid.[11] To obtain an institutional perspective beyond the six schools, we interviewed officials from national organizations representing community colleges, private nonprofit and public colleges and universities, and for-profit schools. A more detailed explanation of our methodology is available in appendix I.

We conducted this performance audit from November 2011 to December 2012 in accordance with generally accepted government auditing standards. Those standards require that we plan and perform the audit to obtain sufficient, appropriate evidence to provide a reasonable basis for our findings and conclusions based on our audit objectives. We believe that the evidence obtained provides a reasonable basis for our findings and conclusions based on our audit objectives.

Background

History of 529 Plans

529 plans are a college savings vehicle that originated in the states. In 1986, Michigan created the Michigan Education Trust to operate what is

---

[11] The College Board is a not-for-profit organization that provides college students with financial aid support and scholarships. It also conducts research and advocacy on behalf of students, educators, schools, and colleges. The PROFILE is a form developed by the College Board to help institutions gather information used to award nonfederal student aid funds.

generally considered the first state prepaid tuition plan. In 1996, Congress enacted Section 529 of the Internal Revenue Code, setting out requirements that state 529 plans must meet to be exempt from federal tax. The Economic Growth and Tax Relief Reconciliation Act of 2001 included a provision making earnings included in distributions from 529 plan accounts entirely tax-exempt as long as they are used to pay for qualified higher education expenses.[12] For other key legislative actions and the value of assets invested in these plans, see fig. 1.

[12] Pub. L. No. 107-16, § 402, 115 Stat. 38, 60. Previously, earnings had been allowed to grow on a tax-deferred basis, but were taxed upon distribution to pay for qualified education expenses.

Figure 1: 529 Plan Timeline and Assets Invested

Year-end assets (in billions of 2012 dollars)

Year	Assets
2001[b]	19.4
2002	33.4
2003	56.2
2004	77.5
2005	94.6
2006	118.8
2007	139.4
2008	110.5
2009	139.2
2010	162.8
2011	167.0

Timeline:

1986 — In what is generally considered the first 529 plan, Michigan creates the Michigan Education Trust to operate a prepaid plan that opens in 1988.

1994 — The U.S. Court of Appeals for the Sixth Circuit rules that investment income from the Michigan Education Trust is not subject to federal income tax.[a]

1996 — Congress enacts section 529 of the Internal Revenue Code, establishing federal rules for 529 plans.

2001 — Economic Growth and Tax Relief Reconciliation Act of 2001 (EGTRRA) makes 529 earnings distributions tax-exempt as long as they are used for qualified education expenses.

2006 — Congress makes permanent the EGTRRA provision that allows for tax-exempt distributions of 529 earnings.[c]

Source: GAO analysis of Financial Research Corporation data and relevant legislation.

Notes:
[a]Michigan v. United States, 40 F.3d 817 (6th Cir. 1994).
[b]We chose to present account data starting in 2001 because the federal tax-exempt status for distributions was granted in 2001 and data were not available for all previous years.
[c]Pension Protection Act of 2006, Pub. L. No. 109-280, tit. XIII § 1304, 120 Stat. 789, 1109.

The number of 529 plan accounts has also increased since the plans were granted expanded federal tax advantages in 2001 (see fig. 2).

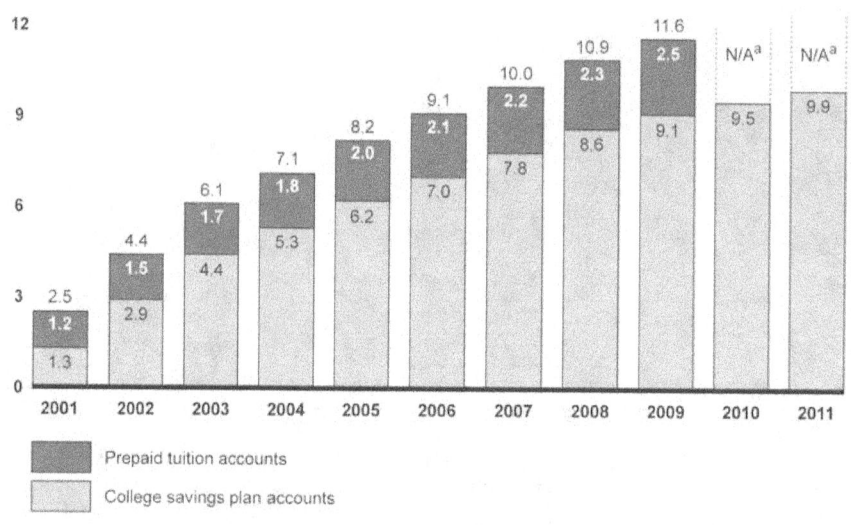

Figure 2: 529 Plan Account Growth

Number of 529 plan accounts (in millions)

Legend:
- Prepaid tuition accounts
- College savings plan accounts

Source: GAO analysis of Financial Research Corporation data.

[a]We did not report prepaid tuition account data for 2010 and 2011 because the method of collecting these data changed in 2009.

Federal Requirements for 529 Plans

529 plans are a state-sponsored investment or savings vehicle whose purpose is to encourage people to save for college.[13] Contributions to 529 plans are made with after-tax dollars and are not deductible for federal tax purposes. Annual contributions in excess of $13,000 are generally subject to federal gift taxes.[14] Total contributions may not exceed the amount necessary to provide for the qualified education expenses of the

---

[13] One additional prepaid plan is not run by a state. The Private College 529 Plan provides a prepaid tuition plan at more than 270 participating private colleges and universities. The Economic Growth and Tax Relief Reconciliation Act of 2001 amended section 529 to provide that one or more eligible educational institutions could establish and maintain a prepaid tuition plan. Prior to that amendment, qualified tuition programs were defined as those established and maintained by a state or state agency or instrumentality.

[14] Contributors may elect to treat contributions between $13,000 and $65,000 as having been made over a 5 calendar-year period without being subject to federal gift taxes.

beneficiary, which is determined by each state; however, individuals may open 529 plan accounts in multiple states.[15] Earnings on contributions grow tax-deferred. When a distribution is made from a 529 plan, the earnings portion is tax-exempt as long as it is used to pay for qualified education expenses.[16] Taxpayers must report to the Internal Revenue Service (IRS) whether the distribution was for qualified higher education expenses. Distributions not used for qualified higher education expenses can be made to either the account owner or beneficiary, but the portion of the nonqualified distribution consisting of investment earnings is taxable and subject to an additional 10 percent penalty.[17] The federal penalty does not apply in some circumstances, for example if the distribution was considered nonqualified because the beneficiary died or received a scholarship.

While section 529 provides that account owners and beneficiaries may not directly or indirectly control how contributions or earnings are invested, in 2001, IRS issued a notice setting out a rule permitting a change in investment strategy once per year and upon a change in the designated beneficiary of the account.[18] For 2009 only, this was increased to twice per year.[19]

There are few federal restrictions on 529 plan participation. For example, there are no income limits and almost anyone can initially be named as a beneficiary—an individual may open a 529 plan account for a child, grandchild, friend, spouse, or for themselves. Further, the 529 plan account owner may change the beneficiary at any time, though the

---

[15] According to CSPN data, overall contribution limits ranged from $235,000 to $400,000 as of July 2012. However, there is no limit on the number of accounts for which an individual can be named the beneficiary. According to a 2009 Treasury report, *An Analysis of Section 529 College Savings and Prepaid Tuition Plans*, a beneficiary can have accounts in as many as 44 states, with effectively no limit on the overall 529 account balance.

[16] An American Opportunity or Lifetime Learning Tax Credit can be claimed in the same year the beneficiary takes a tax-exempt distribution from a 529 plan as long as the same expenses are not used for both benefits.

[17] Qualified education expenses must be reduced by any tax-free educational assistance, such as the tax-free part of scholarships and fellowships, veterans' education assistance, Pell grants, and employer-provided education assistance.

[18] IRS Notice 2001-55.

[19] IRS Notice 2009-1.

subsequent beneficiary must be a member of the family of the original beneficiary in order for this change to be tax-exempt.[20]

529 Plan Operation and Features

Because 529 plans are state-sponsored investments, states determine whether and what type of plans to offer (i.e., prepaid tuition or savings) as well as the eligibility criteria (for example, at the time of application prepaid tuition plans may require either the account owner or beneficiary to be a resident of the state administering the plan whereas residents and nonresidents can invest in most states' college savings plans); administrative and investment fees; and associated state tax benefits. Almost all states offer a college savings plan.[21] In these plans, individuals purchase interests or shares in a trust established by the state. In most cases, the trust assets are invested in mutual funds. The shares in college savings plans can be sold directly by the state or through an external program manager hired by the state (direct-sold) as well as through a financial advisor or broker (advisor-sold). College savings plans may offer a number of investment options, which often include stock mutual funds, bond mutual funds, and money market funds. These investment options can vary in terms of risk and return, ranging, for example, from investments that are insured by the Federal Deposit Insurance Corporation (FDIC) to options that are almost completely invested in aggressive-growth funds. Many plans offer age-based portfolios that shift automatically into more conservative investments as the beneficiary approaches college age. Fifteen states also offer prepaid tuition plans to their state residents.[22] To help run their plans, states may employ marketing staff, advisors, financial consultants, or other experts.

---

[20] A member of the beneficiary's family is defined as including a father, mother, brother, sister, child, grandchild, niece/nephew, son/daughter-in-law, spouse of any individual listed above, and a first cousin, among others.

[21] Wyoming no longer operates its own plan and has entered into an agreement with Colorado's college savings plan whereby Wyoming residents participate under the same terms as Colorado residents. Washington only offers a prepaid tuition plan.

[22] As of July 2012, of the 15 states with prepaid tuition plans, 3 are no longer accepting new enrollees. Kentucky and South Carolina's prepaid tuition plans are currently closed to new enrollments. Tennessee also closed its prepaid tuition plan to new enrollees and contributions in 2010 due to the cost of tuition increasing faster than investment returns. However, it launched a new college savings plan in September 2012.

Some states offer a variety of tax advantages that can include a state deduction or non-refundable credit for plan contributions and tax-deferred earnings.[23] These benefits may apply only to residents who make contributions to their own state's plan or, in a few states, may include contributions made to other states' plans.[24]

Plan Disclosures

Although most 529 college savings plans have been modeled after mutual funds, 529 plans are regulated differently than mutual funds under the federal securities laws because they are regulated as municipal securities.[25] As municipal securities, 529 plans are exempt from the registration and reporting requirements of the federal securities laws.[26] However, broker-dealers selling 529 plans (advisor-sold plans) must comply with the rules of the Municipal Securities Rulemaking Board (MSRB).[27] Specifically, MSRB requires broker-dealers who sell 529 plans to follow certain guidelines, such as having reasonable grounds to believe that the recommended product is suitable for the customer; disclosing certain information, such as plan fees and state tax implications; following certain requirements when advertising; and posting disclosure documents on its Electronic Municipal Market Access Website.[28] However, MSRB rules do not apply to state issuers when they market their 529 plans

---

[23] Tax credits reduce tax filers' income tax liability on a dollar-for-dollar basis. A nonrefundable credit can reduce the amount of taxes owed (tax liability) to zero but not below. A refundable credit can reduce the tax liability to zero and the remaining credit is paid to the taxpayer as a refund. Tax deductions permit tax filers to subtract the applicable contribution amount from income that would otherwise be taxable. Therefore, deductions reduce filers' tax liability less than credits for any given amount claimed.

[24] Arizona, Kansas, Maine, Missouri, and Pennsylvania extend the same state tax benefits to residents who invest in either their own state's 529 plan or another state's plan.

[25] Municipal securities are issued by states and political subdivisions or agencies of states. Prepaid tuition plans are generally not considered municipal securities.

[26] See Section 3(a)(2) of the Securities Act of 1933 and section 3(a)(29) of the Securities Exchange Act of 1934. Disclosures provided in connection with the sale of 529 plans are, however, subject to the antifraud provisions of the federal securities laws.

[27] MSRB establishes standards of fair practice, disclosure, and suitability and professional qualifications for broker-dealers.

[28] While MSRB has the authority, subject to Securities and Exchange Commission (SEC) approval, to establish such standards, it does not enforce its own rules. MSRB rules are enforced against broker-dealers by the Financial Industry Regulatory Authority, a self-regulatory organization that is subject to SEC oversight, and by SEC.

directly to the investor without the assistance of a broker-dealer (direct-sold plans). In 2004, in response to concerns that 529 plan disclosures were inadequate, CSPN, after working with the Securities and Exchange Commission, the MSRB, and the National Association of Securities Dealers, developed voluntary disclosure principles to be adopted by state issuers on plan performance, fees, and state tax information, among other things. These principles were designed to enhance investors' ability to compare information across plans. Since 2004, the principles have been updated several times with the most recent update in May 2011.

Student Financial Aid

As authorized under Title IV of the Higher Education Act of 1965, as amended, the Department of Education provides assistance to help millions of students and families meet the costs of higher education through grants, work-study, and loans. A substantial portion of this federal financial aid is awarded based on the amount of a student's financial need, which is generally the difference between a student's cost of attendance and an estimate of his family's ability to pay these costs, known as the expected family contribution (EFC). In addition to the student's income and assets, parents' income and assets are also used to determine the student's EFC unless the student is classified as independent. Independent students have their income and assets included in the EFC and their spouses' income and assets, if applicable. Several criteria are used to determine if a student is independent, such as the student's age, and if he or she is married or separated, enrolled in a master's or doctoral degree program, or serving on active duty in the military, among other things.

To apply for federal financial aid, students and, in the case of dependent students, parents submit information on income, assets, and the number of children enrolled in college through the Free Application for Federal Student Aid (FAFSA). This information is then used to determine the student's eligibility for federal student aid by calculating the EFC through a process known as federal methodology, which is set out in statute.[29] In terms of assets, figure 3 shows the information required[30] by the FAFSA

---

[29] The methodology for determining the federal EFC is found in Part F of Title IV of the Higher Education Act of 1965, as amended, codified at 20 U.S.C. §§ 1087kk – 1087vv.

[30] Assets that are not required to be reported on the FAFSA include principal place of residence, a family farm, family-owned small businesses, retirement plans, and whole life insurance.

regarding the net worth of students' and parents' investments, which includes savings in 529 plans along with other investments such as Coverdells, money market funds, stocks, and mutual funds (for a full copy of the FAFSA see app. II).[31]

Figure 3: FAFSA Questions on Student and Parent Assets, Including 529 Plans

Free Application for Federal Student Aid

Student's contribution (page 4)

40. As of today, what is your (and spouse's) total current balance of cash, savings and checking accounts? **Don't include** student financial aid. $

41. As of today, what is the net worth of your (and spouse's) investments, including real estate? **Don't include** the home you live in. Net worth means current value minus debt. **See Notes page 2.** $

42. As of today, what is the net worth of your (and spouse's) current businesses and/or investment farms? **Don't include** a family farm or family business with 100 or fewer full-time or full-time equivalent employees. **See Notes page 2.** $

Parents' contribution (page 7)

88. As of today, what is your parents' total current balance of cash, savings and checking accounts? $

89. As of today, what is the net worth of your parents' investments, including real estate? **Don't include** the home in which your parents live. Net worth means current value minus debt. **See Notes page 2.** $

90. As of today, what is the net worth of your parents' current businesses and/or investment farms? **Don't include** a family farm or family business with 100 or fewer full-time or full-time equivalent employees. **See Notes page 2.** $

Notes (page 2)

Notes for questions 41 and 42 (page 4) and 89 and 90 (page 7)

Net worth means current value minus debt. If net worth is negative, enter 0.

Investments include real estate (do not include the home you live in), trust funds, UGMA and UTMA accounts, money market funds, mutual funds, certificates of deposit, stocks, stock options, bonds, other securities, installment and land sale contracts (including mortgages held), commodities, etc.

Investments also include qualified educational benefits or education savings accounts (e.g., Coverdell savings accounts, 529 college savings plans and the refund value of 529 prepaid tuition plans). For a student who does not report parental information, the accounts owned by the student (and/or the student's spouse) are reported as student investments in question 41. For a student who must report parental information, the accounts are reported as parental investments in question 89, including all accounts owned by the student and all accounts owned by the parents for any member of the household.

Source: GAO excerpt from the Free Application for Federal Student Aid, July 1, 2012 – June 30, 2013.

States and institutions may also offer financial aid. To determine the amount of such aid, some states and institutions choose to gather information in addition to what is required by the FAFSA. One form used by some institutions is the College Board's PROFILE form. The PROFILE

---

[31] Prepaid plans are worth the refund value of the credits or certificates.

asks for information not included on the FAFSA, such as home equity and medical expenses, as well as more detail about information that is included on the FAFSA. The institutions may then use an individualized institutional methodology to determine the student's EFC for institutional financial aid.[32]

Few Families Have 529 Plans and Those Who Do Tend to Be Wealthier

A Small Percentage of Families Have 529 Plans

According to the 2010 Survey of Consumer Finances (SCF), less than 3 percent of U.S. families had 529 plans[33] or Coverdells, a similar but less often used education savings account.[34] Even among families who acknowledged upcoming education expenses, 529 plans were not widely used. Of the approximately 25 percent of families who said they expected major education expenses in 5-10 years, about 7 percent of them had 529 plans or Coverdells. Similarly, of the approximately 18 percent of families who reported saving for education was a priority, only about 9 percent had 529 plans or Coverdells. 529 plans are also less commonly

---

[32] Institutional methodology is a College Board formula developed by financial aid professionals, in consultation with economists, to measure a family's ability to pay for college. A basic principle of institutional methodology is the idea that a family's capacity to pay is a function of income and assets.

[33] The SCF asks about survey respondents and members of their households (sometimes referred to as primary economic units), which we refer to as families. About 88 percent of families with 529 plans or Coverdells had children 25 years of age or younger living with them. Among the approximately 39 percent of all families that had children under 25 living with them, only about 6 percent had 529 plans or Coverdells.

[34] The SCF combines responses for 529 plans and Coverdells. Because officials from the Federal Reserve, the federal agency that sponsors the SCF, said respondents did not necessarily distinguish between Coverdells and 529 plans, we did not separate the two account types. However, the officials indicated that a larger share of SCF respondents reported having 529 plans than Coverdells. Further, using SOI data, we estimate that in 2010 approximately 85 percent of tax filers who took a distribution from either a 529 plan or a Coverdell reported distributions from a 529 plan while 14 percent reported distributions from a Coverdell and 1 percent reported distributions from both.

used than other savings vehicles among those saving for college.[35] For example, a 2010 Sallie Mae survey found that most parents saved for college in general savings accounts or certificates of deposit and, of those who did invest, more used general investment vehicles than 529 plans.[36] Based on our analysis of SCF data, the median amount in 529 plan or Coverdell accounts was about $14,700.[37]

Families with 529 Plans Generally Have More Wealth and Education than Those without 529 Plans

Families with 529 plans or Coverdells typically had much more wealth than families without these accounts, according to our analysis of SCF data. Based on our analysis of the 2010 SCF, we estimate that the median financial asset[38] value for families with 529 plans or Coverdells was about $413,500, which is about twenty-five times the median financial asset value for families without 529 plans or Coverdells (about $15,400).[39] For example, families with 529 plans or Coverdells had more retirement assets than other families. Of families with 529 plans or

---

[35] There are other vehicles with tax benefits that can be used for education savings. Such vehicles include Coverdells, funds under the Uniform Gift to Minors Act and Uniform Transfer to Minors Act, individual retirement accounts, and savings bonds.

[36] Information is reported for parents of children younger than 18 who believed their child is likely to attend college and who were saving for this purpose. The survey also found that nearly a quarter of these parents saved for college in retirement savings accounts such as a 401(k) or individual retirement account. Sallie Mae, *How America Saves for College: Sallie Mae's National Study of Parents with Children under 18 Conducted by Gallup* (Reston, VA: 2010).

[37] We are 95 percent confident that the median amount in these accounts was between $9,300 and $20,100. Because Coverdells had annual contribution limits of $2,000 in 2010, this estimate may understate the median amount in 529 plans. However, other data sources have similar findings specific to amounts saved in 529 plan accounts. For instance, in 2011 the College Savings Plan Network reported that the average amount in 529 savings plans was $15,492 in 2010. Unless otherwise noted, all SCF percentage estimates have 95 percent confidence intervals within 5 percentage points of the estimate itself.

[38] Financial assets include, among other things, resources in 529 plans, checking and savings accounts, stocks, bonds, and retirement accounts. See appendix I for more detail.

[39] We are 95 percent confident that the median financial asset value for families with 529 plans or Coverdells was between $247,400 and $579,600. For families without 529 plans or Coverdells, the 95 percent confidence interval is between $13,700 and $17,100.

Coverdells, about 94 percent had retirement assets,[40] such as those in 401(k) accounts or traditional pensions.[41] In contrast, approximately 49 percent of families without 529 plans or Coverdells had these retirement assets. Further, the median value of retirement assets was much greater for those with 529 plans or Coverdells. Specifically, the median value in retirement accounts was about $213,600 for families with 529 plans or Coverdells, while the median value for families without 529 plans or Coverdells was about $40,300.[42] A larger share of families with 529 plans or Coverdells (27 percent) also believed they will have more than enough retirement income from pensions and Social Security to maintain current living standards than the share of families without 529 plans or Coverdells (16 percent), which may put them in a better position to save for college.[43]

Further, the median income of families with 529 plans or Coverdells was about three times the median income of families without these accounts.[44] Specifically, families with 529 plans or Coverdells had median incomes of about $142,400 per year compared to $45,100 for other families.[45] Moreover, we estimate that 47 percent of families with 529 plans or Coverdells had incomes over $150,000, compared to 8 percent for

---

[40] For our purposes, retirement assets include those in defined contribution plans (e.g. retirement savings plans such as a 401(k)), individual retirement accounts, and defined benefit plans from which the participant has the option to borrow or withdraw for both the SCF respondent and his/her spouse.

[41] We use the term 'traditional pensions' to refer to defined benefit plans.

[42] We are 95 percent confident that the amount of retirement assets for families with 529 plans or Coverdell accounts was between $149,700 and $277,500, while the amount for families without these accounts was between $37,400 and $43,200.

[43] We are 95 percent confident that the percentage of families with 529 plans or Coverdell accounts who believed they will have more than enough retirement income was between 19.9 and 33.9 percent. For families without 529 plans or Coverdells, the 95 percent confidence interval was between 15.1 and 16.9 percent.

[44] In 2012, we reported similar findings using data from the 2007 SCF. GAO-12-560.

[45] Because Coverdell contributors must generally have had a modified adjusted gross income of less than $110,000 per year ($220,000 in the case of a joint return) in 2010, this estimate may understate the median income of families with 529 plans. We are 95 percent confident that the median income for families with 529 plans or Coverdells was between $125,400 and $159,400.

families without these accounts (see fig. 4).[46] In 2009, Treasury reported that participation in 529 plans is likely to increase with income, in part, because the tax benefits and overall savings rates increase with income.[47] (For more information see text box on 529 plan savings, below).

Figure 4: Distribution of Income for Families with and without 529 Plans or Coverdells (from SCF)

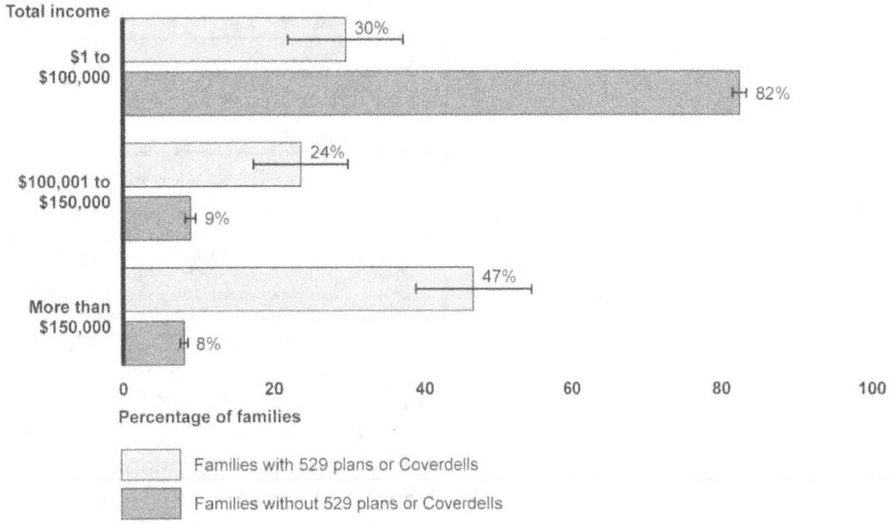

Total income

$1 to $100,000	30% / 82%
$100,001 to $150,000	24% / 9%
More than $150,000	47% / 8%

Percentage of families (0, 20, 40, 60, 80, 100)

☐ Families with 529 plans or Coverdells
▨ Families without 529 plans or Coverdells

Source: GAO analysis of SCF 2010 data.

Notes: Numbers may not add to 100 percent due to rounding. Error bars in the graph display the 95 percent confidence intervals for these estimates. We are 95 percent confident that the percentage of families with 529 plans or Coverdells who have incomes of $1 to $100,000 was between 21.9 and 37.1 percent, that those who have incomes of $100,001 to $150,000 was between 17.4 and 29.8 percent, and that those who have incomes over $150,000 was between 38.8 and 54.4 percent. We are 95 percent confident that the percentage of families without 529 plans or Coverdells who have incomes of $1 to $100,000 was between 81.5 and 83.3 percent, that those who have incomes of $100,001 to $150,000 was between 8.3 and 9.7 percent, and that those who have incomes over $150,000 was between 7.6 and 8.6 percent.

---

[46] We are 95 percent confident that that the percentage of families with 529 plans or Coverdells who have incomes over $150,000 was between 38.8 and 54.4. For families without 529 plans or Coverdells, the 95 percent confidence interval was between 7.6 and 8.6 percent.

[47] The Department of the Treasury, *An Analysis of Section 529 College Savings and Prepaid Tuition Plans: A Report Prepared by the Department of Treasury for the White House Task Force on Middle Class Working Families* (Washington, D.C.: September 9, 2009).

> ### 529 Plan Federal Tax Savings
>
> Using IRS taxpayer data and a microsimulation model from the National Bureau of Economic Research (NBER), we found that taxpayers with higher incomes both took larger distributions from 529 plans and received a larger tax benefit from those distributions (see table below). As we reported in 2012, 529 plan tax incentives are more beneficial to families with higher tax liabilities, in part, because these families have a higher marginal tax rate (see GAO-12-560).
>
> **Distributions and Estimated Federal Tax Savings of 529 Plans in 2010 by Income**
>
> | Total income | Median distribution | Median tax savings |
> | --- | --- | --- |
> | $1 to $100,000 | $7,491 | $561 |
> | $100,001 to $150,000 | $13,394 | $1,958 |
> | Over $150,000 | $18,039 | $3,132 |
>
> Source: GAO analysis of IRS SOI 2010 data using NBER's TAXSIM Model, a microsimulation model.
>
> Notes: We are 95 percent confident that in 2010: the median distribution was between $6,261 and $8,280 and the median tax savings was between $493 and $664 for taxpayers whose total income was between $1 and $100,000; the median distribution was between $10,327 and $16,110 and the median tax savings was between $1,587 and $2,456 for taxpayers whose total income was between $100,001 and $150,000; and the median distribution was between $16,280 and $20,107 and the median tax savings was between $2,858 and $3,415 for taxpayers whose total income was more than $150,000.

As higher-income families tend to have higher levels of education, it is logical that the wealthier families who save in 529 plans or Coverdells also have higher educational attainment than other families. Specifically, about 91 percent of SCF respondents with 529 plans or Coverdells indicated that either they or their spouse/partner had at least a college degree, compared to about 44 percent of families without these accounts. Further, because families with 529 plans have higher education levels, children in these families may be more likely to attend college in the first place as research shows that when parents have obtained a college degree, their children are more likely to attend college.[48]

Also, a larger proportion of respondents in families who had 529 plans or Coverdells were non-minorities, according to our analysis of SCF data.[49] Specifically, about 84 percent of respondents whose families had 529

---

[48] For example, see OECD (2012), *Education at a Glance 2012: OECD Indicators,* OECD Publishing. Accessed on September 11, 2012. http://dx.doi.org/10.1787/eag-2012-en.

[49] Research shows that racial or ethnic minorities are more likely to be low-income, which is a risk factor that may be associated with less positive educational outcomes and can affect educational achievement.

plans or Coverdells identified as white (non-Hispanic).[50] In contrast, about 69 percent of respondents in families without these accounts said they were white (non-Hispanic). Moreover, only 5 percent of respondents in families with 529 plans or Coverdells identified as Black/African-American, compared to 14 percent without these accounts. While SCF does not provide insight on why more white families use 529 plans than others, a 2010 Sallie Mae study found that a larger percentage of white parents saved for college in general when compared to African-American and Hispanic parents. Further, the study found that white families save more for college even when controlling for income.

To determine how the characteristics of families with 529 plans relate to families who already have students in college, we reviewed characteristics of college students' families using data from the 2007-2008 NPSAS.[51] While families with 529 plans are not directly comparable to families of college students,[52] we developed profiles of these two groups to understand the broad trends and found several differences. When compared to families with students already in college, families with 529 plans or Coverdells still tended to have higher income and more education (see table 1).[53] This tendency persisted even when examining the median incomes of dependent and independent students separately. Specifically, median parental income for dependent students was slightly more than half the median income of families with 529 plans or Coverdells, and independent students had slightly more than one-quarter of the median income of those with 529 plans or Coverdells.

---

[50] The family may be multi-racial or mixed race, which is not captured in these data. For example, the respondent's spouse/partner may have a different race or ethnicity. We are 95 percent confident that the percentage of respondents whose families had 529 plans or Coverdells who identified as white (non-Hispanic) was between 78.2 and 88.8 percent.

[51] These were the most recent NPSAS data available.

[52] While our estimates using SCF are for all families (including families with children in college, with children not in college, and with no children), our estimates for families using NPSAS are exclusively for families with a current college student. In NPSAS, families include the student and the student's parents (if the student is dependent) or the student's spouse (if the student is independent). Further, the population of NPSAS students' families is not the same as the population of families with a child in college because a family may have more than one student in college in a given year. Consequently students' family characteristics derived from NPSAS are not directly comparable to family characteristics based on the SCF.

[53] Data were not available on the financial assets held by families of college students.

Table 1: Estimates of Selected Characteristics of College Students' Families (from NPSAS) and Families with and without 529 Plans (from SCF)

| Characteristic | College students' families (from NPSAS) | All Families (from SCF) | |
		Families with 529 plans or Coverdells	Families without 529 plans or Coverdells
Median income[a]	$47,747	$142,400	$45,100
Percent with at least a college degree[b]	42%	91%	44%
Percent white (non-Hispanic)[c]	62%	84%	69%

Source: GAO analysis of NPSAS 2007-2008 and SCF 2010 data.

Notes: All amounts are in 2010 dollars. Unless otherwise noted, percentage estimates have 95 percent confidence intervals within 5 percentage points of the estimate, and median income estimates have 95 percent confidence intervals within 5 percent of the estimate itself.

[a]For college students' families, this is the students' parents' income (for dependent students) or the students' income including their spouses' if married (for independent students). For "all families", this is the total household income. We are 95 percent confident that the median income for families with 529 plans or Coverdells was between $125,400 and $159,400.

[b]For college students' families, this is the percentage of students who had at least one parent with a college degree. For "all families", this is the percentage of families in which the respondent or his/her spouse or partner had at least a college degree.

[c]For college students' families, this is the percentage of students with this race/ethnicity. For "all families", this is the percentage of families for which the respondent had this race/ethnicity. We are 95 percent confident that the percentage of respondents whose families had 529 plans or Coverdells who identified as white (non-Hispanic) was between 78.2 and 88.8 percent.

For additional information on 529 plan distributions, see text box below.

---

529 Plan Distributions

In 2010, more than 1 million taxpayers reported taking approximately $23.8 billion in distributions from 529 plans, which they generally reported using for qualified education expenses. Our review of IRS data found that about 5 percent of taxpayers who took distributions from a 529 plan reported that a portion of their 529 plan distributions were nonqualified and subject to a penalty. See table below for additional data.

	2007	2008	2009	2010
Number of taxpayers taking distributions from 529 plans (in millions)	0.82	0.97	1.07	1.08
Total amount of distributions from 529 plans (in billions of 2010 dollars)	$8.5	$19.1	$20.5	$23.8
Percent of taxpayers for which some portion of the 529 plan distribution was reported as nonqualified and subject to a penalty	7.8%	6.7%	6%	5.3%

Source: GAO analysis of IRS SOI 2007-2010 data.

Notes: We are 95 percent confident that the number of taxpayers who reported taking distributions from 529 plans was between 772,000 and 867,000 in 2007, between 916,000 and 1,019,000 in 2008, between 1,012,000 and 1,127,000 in 2009, and between 1,023,000 and 1,135,000 in 2010. We are 95 percent confident that the total amount of 529 plan distributions (in 2010 dollars) was between $7.8 and $9.2 billion in 2007, between $17.7 and $20.5 billion in 2008, between $18.9 and $22.2 billion in 2009, and between $21.2 and $26.4 billion in 2010.

States' 529 Plan Features and Other Factors Can Affect Participation

Tax Benefits, Fees, and Investment Options Vary Across State 529 Plans

Officials in every state and most experts and representatives we interviewed identified tax benefits, fees, and investment options as some of the most important features consumers consider when choosing whether or not to participate in a 529 plan and, if so, which plan to choose. These features vary by state and plan.[54] All states offer at least one plan and many offer a combination of college savings (either direct-sold, advisor-sold, or both) and prepaid plans. For example, 14 states offer a direct-sold plan only, 22 states offer both direct-sold and advisor-sold plans, and 6 states offer all three plan types: direct-sold, advisor-sold, and prepaid. The popularity of direct-sold college savings plans has grown over time and in 2011 total assets were essentially evenly split between those and advisor-sold plans.

State Tax Benefits

States offer a range of tax benefits for 529 plans, and these benefits are a primary incentive to investing in a 529 plan, according to many state officials we interviewed. In addition to earnings growing tax-deferred, our analysis of CSPN data shows the majority of states with an income tax offer some form of benefits: 33 offer a tax deduction and 3 offer a nonrefundable tax credit to residents who participate in their state's plan.[55] Five states also extend benefits to residents who participate in any state's plan. Almost all states limit tax benefits to the account owners, but one state extends those benefits to grandparents, aunts, and uncles who contribute to the plan. Officials in some states we interviewed said they provide additional tax benefits, for example, one state offers an exemption from the state inheritance tax. Others allow contribution amounts that exceed the annual deduction limit to be carried over to the following year's return.[56]

Fees

Various fees and expenses may be associated with 529 plans, including administrative and investment fees. Administrative fees, which are charged by the state and/or the program manager hired by the state,

---

[54] Throughout the report, the term states' plans also includes the plan offered by the District of Columbia.

[55] As of July 2012, 5 states allow residents to deduct all 529 plan contributions in a given tax year. Overall, 28 states provide a tax deduction on contributions, with a variety of limits. Among these states, for example, 18 states allow deductions that range from $500 to $10,000 for a single filer and $1,000 to $20,000 for married couples filing jointly. Additionally, 9 other states also allow deductions—ranging from $250 to $13,000—per beneficiary.

[56] We previously reported tax filers may have difficulty figuring out how to maximize federal tax benefits given interactions with state tax codes. To maximize their combined federal and state tax benefit, tax filers may also need to take into account the state treatment of federal higher education tax expenditures. See GAO-12-560.

cover administration of the 529 program, including customer service and marketing. Investment fees are charged by the investment company to manage the funds. The aggregate of these administrative and investment fees is often referred to as "annual asset-based fees," which are expressed as a percentage of the fund's average net assets. In addition, advisor-sold plans may also charge a "sales load"—that is, a fee paid to the selling broker when the fund is purchased or redeemed—and direct-sold and advisor-sold plans may also charge participants additional fees for services such as enrolling or changing the account owner.

Fees among 529 plans vary widely; total annual asset-based fees among plans nationwide ranged from 0 percent to 1.97 percent for direct-sold plans and 0 percent to 2.78 percent for advisor-sold plans, as of July 2012. As seen in table 2, there is variation among states in both administrative and investment fees. Such variation occurred even among states with similar administrative structures. For example, among three of the states we reviewed where most administrative functions were conducted in-house, one state charged administrative fees of between 0.44 percent and 0.46 percent of the balance annually, another charged between 0.15 percent and 0.20 percent, and a third charged no administrative fees, instead covering operational costs and salaries through an annual state appropriation.[57] Investment fees also varied: for example, underlying mutual fund fees ranged from 0 percent to 1.82 percent of the balance annually, depending on the type of investment option a participant chooses. For advisor-sold funds, sales loads also varied, ranging from 0 percent to 5.75 percent,[58] in part based on the fund class.[59] In addition, among the five states we reviewed, four did not charge an enrollment or application fee, while one charged $25, although the fee may be waived through promotions to encourage participation.

---

[57] A state's administrative fees may vary within a range based on the investment option chosen by the participant.

[58] Initial sales charges are paid when the shares are purchased and deferred sales charges are paid when the shares are redeemed.

[59] Some mutual funds offer investors different types of shares, known as classes. Each class will invest in the same investment portfolio but will have different shareholder services and/or distribution arrangements with different fees and expenses.

Table 2: Fee Ranges (Percent) for College Savings Plans, Direct-Sold and Advisor-Sold

Fee	Description	Range for Direct-Sold Plans (in percent)	Range for Advisor-sold Plans (in percent)
Administrative Fees			
State Fee	Fees charged by the state for operational costs.	0 to 0.75	0 to 0.15
Program Manager Fee	Fee charged by program manager for administering the plan.	0 to 0.8	0 to 1.15
Investment Fees			
Underlying Fund Expense	Expenses or fees charged by an investment firm for managing the funds in the plans.	0 to 1.82	0 to 1.82
Distribution Fee	Fee charged in advisor-sold plans provided to brokers who sold the fund shares.	—	0 to 1.0
Miscellaneous Fees		0 to 0.77	0 to 0.5

Source: GAO analysis of CSPN data as of July 2012.

Note: In addition to the fees listed above, plans may also charge application, cancellation, change in beneficiary, change in investment options, or other fees.

529 plan fees remain higher than fees for similar mutual funds an investor might purchase outside of a 529 plan. According to a 2011 study by Morningstar, 529 plan mutual funds charged, on average, an additional 0.31 percent of the account balance annually in investment fees compared with their respective mutual fund categories in the open market.[60] The administrative fees charged by most 529 funds raise the cost even higher. However, Morningstar does note that fees for 529 plans have declined in recent years and officials at the majority of state plans we interviewed told us they have taken steps to reduce fees – for example, by renegotiating program manager contracts, using competitive bidding for program management, or consolidating functions in-house rather than using a program manager. As we have previously reported, fees are one of many factors participants should consider when investing because even a small fee increase can significantly decrease savings over time.[61]

---

[60] Morningstar, *2011 529 College Savings Plans Research Paper and Industry Survey* (Chicago, IL: October 2011)

[61] GAO, *Private Pensions: Changes Needed to Provide 401(k) Plan Participants and the Department of Labor Better Information on Fees,* GAO-07-21 (Washington, D.C.: November 16, 2006) and *401(k) Plans: Increased Educational Outreach and Broader Oversight May Help Reduce Plan Fees,* GAO-12-325 (Washington, D.C.: April 24, 2012).

Investment Options

State plans offer a variety of investment options to 529 college savings plan participants.[62] Plans in the states we reviewed, for example, include up to 17 different investment options, including age-based, static, and customized portfolios, to cater to participants' various levels of risk tolerance and investment sophistication. Age-based options were generally the most popular and, according to state officials we interviewed, may appeal to investors who might have more limited investment experience or a lower risk tolerance. One state plan we reviewed also offers a customized option for participants who seek more control over their investments, which allows them to designate their own allocations in funds such as stocks and bonds. For more risk-averse participants, some states also offer a FDIC-insured investment option or one that in some other way guarantees the investment's principal.[63] To help investors determine which plan best meets their needs, officials we interviewed in two states said their states provide risk assessment information through customer call centers.[64] One state developed a risk tolerance questionnaire to explain investment scenarios, while the other had a representative ask informal questions to help potential investors assess their own risk level.

Families can also choose to invest in prepaid plans, which were offered in three of the five states we reviewed. These plans also vary in fees, payment options, and cost. Two plans, for example, charged an annual administrative fee of just under 0.50 percent and the third charged no annual fee. In terms of payment options and costs, two states we interviewed offered prepaid plans by academic periods or units that can be used to pay for future tuition costs with the option of paying in lump sum or through a monthly payment program. According to state officials, the cost of these prepaid plans is generally determined by forecasting future tuition and fees at different types of schools (4-year, community college, etc.), given a number of actuarial assumptions on tuition inflation and anticipated investment return. One state, for example, offered a contract to cover four years of college costs for a child currently under

---

[62] In states we reviewed, assets in prepaid plans are invested by the state.

[63] According to CSPN data, 45 states offer age-based investment options and 20 states offer a guaranteed investment option.

[64] While these assessments are designed to help investors decide which plan best meets their risk tolerance and investment goals, state officials told us they do not provide investment advice.

age five at a lump sum of $56,600 and another state offered a similar contract for just under $66,500. A third state we reviewed does not offer units or contracts, but allows participants to contribute any amount to the plan. When the participant withdraws the funds for qualified educational expenses, they will receive the amount they contributed adjusted by a tuition inflation value.

Participation is Affected by Ability to Save and Other Factors, but Some States Have Adopted Strategies to Address Barriers

Families encounter a number of barriers as they consider saving for college: they may struggle with making saving a priority, and for those who do plan to save, many do not know 529 plans exist as a savings option. Additionally, once families decide to invest in a 529 plan they may have trouble understanding how it works and the variation across plans may affect their ability to select one that best meets their needs (see fig. 5).

Figure 5: Factors that Affect 529 Plan Participation

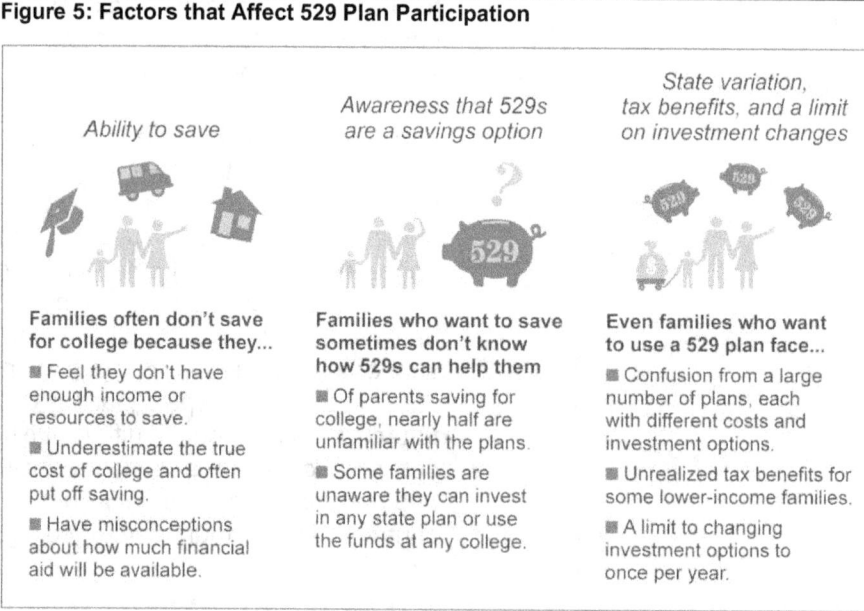

Source: GAO analysis based on reports and interviews with 529 plan officials and experts.

Ability to Save

Families may encounter a variety of barriers saving for college, such as insufficient income, underestimating the cost of college, and misconceptions about financial aid availability, but selected states are taking steps to help address these barriers. A 2010 national survey published by Sallie Mae found that while nearly nine out of ten parents expected their child would attend some form of higher education, only three out of five parents of college-bound children have saved or invested for their oldest child's education.[65]

First, many families may not save because they lack adequate income or have competing financial priorities. The same Sallie Mae survey reported that 68 percent of those who are not saving cited a lack of money as a major reason.[66] State officials and some experts we interviewed also cited this as a challenge: for example, one state official said that the economic downturn has affected some families who are reluctant to make deposits or participate in a 529 plan because they may need to choose between paying their mortgage and saving for college. In terms of competing priorities, two industry representatives we interviewed stressed that retirement should be a higher priority than saving for college. Officials from one state added when a family's budget shrinks or the economy is uncertain, families reduce college rather than retirement savings. Furthermore, a few industry representatives said families should consider using other tax-deferred savings vehicles where funds could be used for multiple purposes, such as retirement and education. The states we selected to review have adopted strategies to expand participation among lower income families who may have limited resources to allocate towards savings, including offering matching programs, low minimum initial contributions, and less risky investment options.

- **Matching Programs:** While a limited number of states offer such options, matching programs to expand low-income families' participation and increase contributions by incentivizing saving have increased this group's participation and college access, according to some state officials we interviewed. According to CSPN data, 14 states offer some form of matching program and two of the three states we reviewed specifically use matching programs to target low-income families. To qualify in one state, for example, a family must earn less than 200 percent of the federal poverty level[67] and deposit a minimum of $100 during the participating calendar year. The state then matches contributions,

---

[65] Sallie Mae, August 2010.

[66] Sallie Mae, August 2010.

[67] For example, in 2011 a family of 4 earning less than $44,700 would qualify, according to plan documentation.

dollar for dollar, up to $400 annually per beneficiary for up to 4 years. In addition to increasing participation, officials from one state plan noted that the matching program can also help minimize student loans and reduce the amount students will have to work while in school. An ongoing experiment conducted by the Center for Social Development also found a positive impact on the number of 529 plan accounts for families who were automatically enrolled in a state-owned 529 account with a matching program in one state.[68] In addition to participating in the automatically opened account, families in the treatment group were offered an additional $100 to open a private account. These families opened private 529 accounts at a higher rate (17 percent of families with a match compared to 2 percent of those in the control group without the incentives), and deposited more into those accounts.[69] While matching programs may have positive results, two states we reviewed reported challenges with funding and awareness. One state's program had not been authorized since 2008 and officials in another state said their enrollment remained low despite being open to all participants because the state's 529 marketing budget was eliminated.

- **Low or No Minimum Initial Contributions:** Low or no minimum initial contributions and fee waivers may also help increase participation among low-income families, according to state officials and others we interviewed. Nationally, minimum initial

---

[68] Center for Social Development, George Warren Brown School of Social Work, Washington University in St. Louis, *The SEED for Oklahoma Kids Experiment: Initial Account Opening and Savings*, (St. Louis, MO: 2010). The study was conducted in partnership with the State of Oklahoma and RTI International. SEED for Oklahoma first automatically enrolled treatment participants who received $1,000 in an Oklahoma 529 account. (Among the 1,361 treatment participants, one declined opening the state-owned account.) These participants were also provided a time-limited incentive of $100 to open their own private accounts, savings matches, and information on Oklahoma 529 accounts. In contrast, control participants were offered no SEED for Oklahoma financial incentives or information about Oklahoma 529, although they could open their own 529 plan accounts, just as any non-study participant. Additional data on participants are expected to be collected over the next few years.

[69] Rates only include additional private accounts opened by participants, i.e. accounts that were separate from the state-owned accounts that were opened automatically for the treatment group. The average deposit amount was $61 for treatment participants and $40 for the control group (not statistically significant). However for the subcategory of private accounts owned by parents or guardians, treatment participants deposited an average of $47 versus $13 for the control group ($p<.05$).

contributions range from $10 to $5,000, according to our analysis of CSPN data; however, the majority of states require an initial contribution of $25 or less. Two states allow participants to open an account with any amount. Officials in one state reported that keeping the initial deposit amounts low can also help facilitate one of their main goals: to help spur the mental commitment and habit to save.

- **Less Risky Investment Options:** Officials from many states we reviewed said they offer investment options that pose less risk to the investor, which can appeal to low- to moderate-income families. One state, for example, partnered with two local banks to provide a FDIC-insured option to target families who might otherwise save in the bank's savings account. According to an official from the plan's banking partner, clients with more assets often use financial planners and are aware of 529 plans, while the FDIC-insured option was designed for those without financial planners and who use the bank's more traditional products.

According to state officials, most of the states we reviewed are not tracking participant's demographic information such as income, however, making the success of these efforts for low-income families difficult to assess.

Second, in addition to insufficient income, some families may not save because they procrastinate or underestimate the true cost of college, according to officials from most of the states we reviewed. Some parents may not budget money to save for college due to a lack of understanding about what college really costs or they become overwhelmed and do nothing, officials at one state 529 plan said. To address these challenges, selected state 529 plans have adopted financial literacy programs and marketing strategies emphasizing the importance of saving even a small amount early and often.[70] To target families with younger children, two states provide materials to parents of newborns through the hospital or direct mail and two states work with elementary schools to distribute materials on the states' 529 plans. Some states also establish contribution deadlines linked to certain benefits, such as discounted enrollment, or provide incentives to families who contribute during certain times of the year. To prevent families from feeling overwhelmed about college costs, one state has focused its marketing on saving a small amount each month, $25, to help reduce the student's future debt, instead of focusing on the total cost of college.

Third, parents may not save for college because they have misconceptions about financial aid availability, according to state officials and some higher education experts. Some noted that families may not understand that most students receive aid in the form of loans that will need to be repaid, rather than receiving grants or scholarships. According to a 2010 national study, 84 percent of non-saving parents expect their child to qualify for enough scholarships or financial aid to cover the costs of college with 49 percent citing it as a major reason for not saving.[71] However, according to our analysis of NPSAS data for all postsecondary students in the 2007-2008 school year, only about half received grants with a median amount of $3,400 (in 2010 dollars). About 40 percent of students took out loans, with a median amount of about $6,800 (in 2010 dollars). Financial aid including grants and loans only covered 37 percent of a student's cost of attendance, with the median out-of-pocket expenses totaling about $7,000 per student (in 2010 dollars). Further, while many families hope to fund college through financial aid, one recent study found that 2011 levels of scholarships were unsustainable as colleges felt the

---

[70] The Department of Education has emphasized the importance of financial literacy related to college savings. For example, the GEAR UP program, where grantees design projects that promote participating students' secondary school completion and enrollment in postsecondary education, also includes promotion of financial literacy and economic literacy education or counseling. In 2012, Education announced a plan to introduce in fiscal year 2013 a new demonstration project, which includes an evaluation component, to determine the effectiveness of pairing federally-supported college savings accounts with GEAR UP activities as part of an overall college access and success strategy. Education has also recently sponsored research assessing interventions that provide families with information on 529 college savings plans and incentives for them to invest in such accounts. The study will gather data on the effects of these interventions on college savings behavior and college outcomes.

[71] Sallie Mae, August 2010.

impact of a difficult economic climate, constraints on endowments, and tighter budgets.[72] In response, many of the states we reviewed have attempted to address misconceptions about the financial aid process. For example, one state lists common myths about 529 plans on its website, explaining that approximately 60 percent of federal financial aid comes in the form of loans, a debt the family must repay. The site encourages families to save even in small amounts to offset the amount of debt the family will incur.

Awareness of 529 Plans as a Savings Option

For those who are saving for college, awareness that 529 plans exist as a savings option is a challenge to participation, according to officials in most of the states we reviewed. In addition, among parents who are saving for college, one study found that almost half are unfamiliar with 529 plans. An additional 4 percent volunteered that they had never heard of the plan or did not know what it was.[73] Families also learn about 529 plans through financial planners, according to many state officials we interviewed; therefore, awareness may be a particular challenge for low-income families who generally do not have access to such resources. Further, some state officials and industry representatives we interviewed encountered families with misperceptions about how 529 plans work, such as not understanding they can invest in plans outside their home state or use savings at any college or university. For example, officials from two states reported families mistakenly believe prepaid plans can only be used at an in-state institution.[74]

State Variation, Tax Implications, and a Limit on Investment Option Changes

While the high number of plans and variation in investment options and cost can offer consumers choice, families who ultimately decide to save with a 529 plan can find it difficult to compare plans, according to many state officials and experts. For example, the wide range of fee types can be difficult to understand and compare across plans because they are not consistent and it is difficult to compare asset-based fees based on percentages with flat fees such as an annual fee in dollar amounts, according to one financial expert. Plan complexity can also make

---

[72] Sallie Mae, *How America Pays for College 2012* (Newark, DE: 2012).

[73] Sallie Mae, August 2010.

[74] If a beneficiary of a prepaid tuition plan elects to attend an out-of-state college, the state 529 plan will typically pay the student's chosen institution the tuition and fees it would have paid at an in-state public college, which may be less than the tuition at the chosen institution.

marketing and communication difficult, according to officials we interviewed in two states. Marketing officials from one state told us consumers requested more information on 529 plans, but it was difficult to communicate information about the complex plans in a simple, consumer-friendly way. Officials in another state noted that plan complexity and a lack of clear information can discourage families from researching and enrolling in a plan.

Many state officials and some academic experts and industry representatives reported that simplifying the information available to consumers might keep families from feeling overwhelmed. Because MSRB rules do not apply to state issuers when they market their direct-sold 529 plans, CSPN developed a set of disclosure principles to help states provide consistent information. The voluntary principles contain recommendations to help consumers understand plans and compare various features, such as fees, tax issues, and risk. While disclosures have been helpful, according to one expert who consults with a number of states, there is room for improvement: disclosures could be more rigorous in ensuring that consumers are informed of less-costly options within a state if they exist and should cover information on prepaid plans, which is currently not standardized. When comparing direct-sold disclosure documents across states we reviewed, we found that the five states generally adhered to the CSPN disclosure principles and contained consistent information a consumer could compare. Three states, however, were missing some information that could be helpful to consumers, such as information on the risk of state tax law changes and a statement that 529 plans should only be used to save for qualified higher education expenses.

The structure of federal and state tax benefits, a primary incentive for some 529 plan investors, can also affect participation as they may not be as helpful to low-income families, according to some academic experts, industry representatives, and state officials we interviewed.[75] Low-income families with low or no tax liability see less benefit from federal tax benefits and may see no benefit from nonrefundable state tax credits provided to 529 plan investors. According to a 2009 Treasury report, families saving in 529 plans may need to carefully consider whether their

---

[75] Prior GAO work has also found education savings accounts, such as 529 plans, are more advantageous to families with higher incomes and tax liabilities. See GAO-12-560.

child will go to college because the penalty incurred if the funds are not used for qualified education expenses may outweigh the tax benefits for low-income families.[76] In addition, Treasury noted most states do not extend tax benefits to residents investing in out-of-state plans, limiting competition. As a result, families have a strong incentive to choose their home state plan even if other plans offer preferable investment choices. In 2009, Treasury recommended states eliminate this "home-state bias" to provide more investment options to consumers, more intense competition between plans, and potentially lower fees.[77] According to an annual report from one state that extends its tax benefits to residents who invest in other states' plans, doing so, when other states do not, puts the home state plan at a competitive disadvantage. State officials explained that this policy results in other plans marketing their products in the state. Residents, therefore, may be unaware of their home state plan's benefits, according to the report.

Finally, the fact that account holders may change their investment option only one time per year may affect participation in 529 plans, according to state officials and some industry representatives we interviewed. Officials from one financial services company advocated removing any limits on changing investment choices beyond those imposed by the financial services company sponsoring the fund, as is the case with 401(k) plans and individual retirement accounts. Another industry representative observed some 529 plan participants changing their account beneficiary solely because it would allow them to change their investment options. However, the representative cautioned that participants should not change their investment options too frequently; many experts advocate that investors are best served by sticking with a long-term investment plan.

---

[76] Treasury, 2009.

[77] Treasury, 2009. In addition, Treasury also recommended increasing the provision of age-based indexed funds; making contribution limits more effective by making them per-beneficiary limits rather than per-beneficiary per-state limits; improving industry reporting of plans' historical returns, plan participation by income, and how plans are invested at the account level; and improving government monitoring of 529 plan accounts and their disbursements.

Savings in 529 Plans Affect Financial Aid the Same as Other Assets

Savings in 529 Plans Are Treated Similarly to Other Assets That Are Included When Calculating the Expected Family Contribution

The extent to which savings in 529 plans, or other investments, affect how much a family is expected to contribute to the cost of college—the federal expected family contribution (EFC)—generally depends on the family's amount of assets. Education incorporates the amount of specific types of assets into various calculations to determine the EFC.[78] However, in two calculations, families who meet certain criteria are either not expected to contribute to the cost of college (automatic zero EFC) or they qualify for a simplified calculation.[79] In both cases, assets, including savings in 529 plans, are not included in the calculation of the EFC. According to the 2007-2008 NPSAS, about a quarter of families who filed FAFSAs met these criteria.

In other calculations, assets, including savings in 529 plans, may affect the EFC to different extents depending on whether students are dependent on their parents or are independent with dependents of their own. For dependent students, between 2.64 percent and 5.64 percent of parental assets may be included in the EFC as described below:

- First, the parents report the net worth (current value minus debt) of their investments (see fig. 6 #1),[80] but before the total contribution from assets is calculated, an amount known as the "education savings and asset protection allowance" is subtracted

---

[78] Assets that are not required to be reported on the FAFSA include principal place of residence, a family farm, family-owned small businesses, retirement plans, and whole life insurance.

[79] Students can qualify for an automatic zero EFC or a simplified EFC based on their parents' income (dependent students) or their income (independent students) and any of the following: (1) receipt of federal benefits, such as Social Security Supplemental Security Income or food stamps, (2) no requirement to file an income tax return or may file an IRS 1040A or 1040EZ, or (3) a parent (dependent student) or student/spouse (independent student) is a dislocated worker.

[80] Prepaid plans are worth the refund value of the tuition credits or certificates.

(see fig. 6, #2). This allowance is designed to help protect a portion of the parents' assets.[81]

- Second, 12 percent of any parental asset amount that exceeds the education savings and asset protection allowance is used to determine the contribution from assets that will be considered in the final EFC calculation (see fig. 6 #3).

- Third, this contribution from assets is added to the parents' available income to determine their adjusted available income (see fig. 6, #4).

- Fourth, a marginal rate, from 22 percent up to a maximum of 47 percent, is applied to the sum of the parents' available income and contributions from assets (known collectively as the adjusted available income) to determine their EFC (see fig. 6, #5). As a result, the amount of net parental assets, including savings in 529 plans, that can be included in the EFC ranges from 2.64 percent to 5.64 percent.[82]

---

[81] The education savings and asset protection allowance increases with the age of the older parent. For example, in the 2012-2013 school year, the allowance for two parents, the older of which was 45, was $41,300 whereas the allowance for two parents, the older of which was 55, was $53,400. According to Education's Federal Student Aid Handbook, the allowances approximate the present cost of an annuity, which, when combined with Social Security benefits, would provide at age 65 a moderate level of living for a retired couple or single person.

[82] The 2.64 percent is the result of assessing 22 percent of the 12 percent of assets that are included in the EFC ($.22 \times .12 = .0264$). Similarly, 5.64 percent results from assessing 47 percent of 12 percent ($.47 \times .12 = .0564$).

Figure 6: Expected Family Contribution from Parents' Assets for Dependent Student

EFC formula workbook (page 9)

PARENTS' CONTRIBUTION FROM ASSETS		
16. Cash, savings & checking (FAFSA/SAR #88)		
17. Net worth of investments** (FAFSA/SAR #89) If negative, enter zero.		
18. Net worth of business and/or investment farm (FAFSA/SAR #90) If negative, enter zero.		
19. Adjusted net worth of business/farm (Calculate using Table A4.)	+	
20. Net worth (sum of lines 16, 17, and 19)	=	
21. Education savings and asset protection allowance (Table A5)	−	
22. Discretionary net worth (line 20 minus line 21)	=	
23. Asset conversion rate	×	.12
24. CONTRIBUTION FROM ASSETS If negative, enter zero.	=	

PARENTS' CONTRIBUTION		
AVAILABLE INCOME (AI) (from line 15)		
CONTRIBUTION FROM ASSETS (from line 24)	+	
25. Adjusted Available Income (AAI) May be a negative number.	=	
26. Total parents' contribution from AAI (Calculate using Table A6.) If negative, enter zero.	=	
27. Number in college in 2012-2013 (Exclude parents) (FAFSA/SAR #73)	+	
28. PARENTS' CONTRIBUTION (standard contribution for nine-month enrollment)*** If negative, enter zero.	=	

1 Net worth of parental investments are reported.

2 Education savings and asset protection allowance is subtracted.

3 All parental assets, including savings in 529 plans, are initially assessed at a rate of 12 percent.

4 This contribution from assets is added to the available income to determine the adjusted available income.

5 A marginal rate, from 22 percent to 47 percent, is applied to the adjusted available income to determine the parents' contribution. Thus, the amount of parents' assets that can be assessed in their expected family contribution ranges from 2.64 percent to 5.64 percent.

Source: GAO analysis of Education's *The EFC Formula, 2012-2013.*

Even if the dependent student is the 529 plan account owner, the savings are still assessed at the parents' asset rate. The EFC includes 20 percent of the value of a dependent student's assets; however, savings in a 529 plan where the student is the account owner are still considered assets of the dependent student's parent(s).

Independent students can have up to 20 percent of their 529 plans savings and other assets included in their EFC. However, assets of independent students with dependents (other than a spouse) may be assessed at a lower rate. After an asset protection allowance is subtracted from their net assets, any remainder is multiplied by 7 percent. Then, a marginal rate, from 22 percent to 47 percent, is applied to the sum of their available income and contribution from assets—similar to the process used for parental assets of dependents students. Therefore, from 1.54 percent to 3.29 percent of assets may be included in their EFC. In contrast, independent students who do not have dependents (other than a spouse) will have 20 percent of any assets exceeding the asset protection allowance included in their EFC. Education officials said independent students without children to support are generally expected to contribute a higher percentage of their assets because their primary focus should be on paying for their education.

Distributions from 529 plans owned by parents and/or the student will not be considered as income in the EFC calculation in future years if they are used for qualified education expenses. However, if a student receives 529 plan distributions from an account owned by someone other than himself or the custodial parent, those funds count as student income and could affect the EFC in subsequent years.[83] For example, if a student received funds from a 529 plan owned by a grandparent, he would have to report those funds as untaxed student income on the next year's FAFSA, according to Education officials (see fig. 7).

---

[83] Since the EFC is based on the previous year's income, distributions from a 529 plan not owned by the parent or student would not affect the EFC for the student's last year in college if the student received the funds after his final FAFSA had been filed.

Figure 7: FAFSA Questions on Student Untaxed Income

Student's financial information (page 5)

44. Student's 2011 Untaxed Income (Enter the combined amounts for you and your spouse.)

a. Payments to tax-deferred pension and savings plans (paid directly or withheld from earnings), including, but not limited to, amounts reported on the W-2 forms in Boxes 12a through 12d, codes D, E, F, G, H and S.

b. IRA deductions and payments to self-employed SEP, SIMPLE, Keogh and other qualified plans from IRS Form 1040—line 28 + line 32 or 1040A—line 17.

c. Child support received for any of your children. **Don't include** foster care or adoption payments.

d. Tax exempt interest income from IRS Form 1040—line 8b or 1040A—line 8b.

e. Untaxed portions of IRA distributions from IRS Form 1040—lines (15a minus 15b) or 1040A—lines (11a minus 11b). Exclude rollovers. If negative, enter a zero here.

f. Untaxed portions of pensions from IRS Form 1040—lines (16a minus 16b) or 1040A—lines (12a minus 12b). Exclude rollovers. If negative, enter a zero here.

g. Housing, food and other living allowances paid to members of the military, clergy and others (including cash payments and cash value of benefits). **Don't include** the value of on-base military housing or the value of a basic military allowance for housing.

h. Veterans noneducation benefits, such as Disability, Death Pension, or Dependency & Indemnity Compensation (DIC) and/or VA Educational Work-Study allowances.

i. Other untaxed income not reported in items 44a through 44h, such as workers' compensation, disability, etc. Also include the first-time homebuyer tax credit from IRS Form 1040—line 67. **Don't include** student aid, earned income credit, additional child tax credit, welfare payments, untaxed Social Security benefits, Supplemental Security Income, Workforce Investment Act educational benefits, on-base military housing or a military housing allowance, combat pay, benefits from flexible spending arrangements (e.g., cafeteria plans), foreign income exclusion or credit for federal tax on special fuels.

j. Money received, or paid on your behalf (e.g., bills), not reported elsewhere on this form.

Line 44j is where students report as untaxed income any distributions that did not come from either their own or their parents' 529 plan.

Source: GAO excerpt from the Free Application for Federal Student Aid, July 1, 2012 – June 30, 2013.

A small percentage of families who applied for federal financial aid in 2007-2008 had enough assets to be included in the determination of their EFC. In our analysis of families who filled out the FAFSA, we found that 13 percent of all students—24 percent of dependent students and 4 percent of independent students—had enough assets to be included in their EFC.[84] In other words, the net worth of their (and possibly their parents' or spouses') assets exceeded the savings and asset protection allowance and was included in the EFC at some percentage. Education officials said that because the asset protection allowance is high, federal student aid decisions do not heavily rely on assets, such as savings in 529 plans. Officials told us that while home equity was removed from the list of assets used to calculate the EFC in 1992, the asset protection allowance remained the same. Since then, they said, assets have been a less relevant factor in calculating the EFC.

---

[84] In 2007-2008, 61 percent of dependent and 52 percent of independent students filled out the FAFSA.

Many States and Selected Institutions Also Treat 529 Plan Savings As Assets

States

Most state financial aid offices also consider savings in 529 plans as assets.[85] According to the 2009-2010 National Association of State Student Grant and Aid Programs survey,[86] 35 states reported that they used the federal methodology for determining the EFC for state aid.[87] However, some states that reported using federal methodology for their primary student needs analysis also indicated they provide special treatment for state 529 college savings or prepaid plans when determining student eligibility for aid. Specifically, seven states that used federal methodology to award their state aid excluded the state's 529 college savings plan and three excluded the state's prepaid plan from their calculation for state aid.

Of the officials in the six state financial aid offices we interviewed, none said they considered assets to a greater extent than the FAFSA and a few said their state took specific steps to exempt savings in these plans from consideration. Specifically, officials in two states said there is language in their 529 plan authorizing legislation that exempts plan savings when determining a student's eligibility for state financial aid. Officials in another state said their state issued a regulation stating that savings in a 529 plan would not affect state grant eligibility for residents attending nonprofit higher education institutions. An official in a fourth state said the legislature changed its higher education authorization language so that students would still be eligible to receive a state scholarship even if they enrolled in the state's prepaid plan.

Institutions

Institutional financial aid practices vary with regard to assets, but those with more aid to award may gather additional information about a family's financial status, according to some representatives of national financial

---

[85] According to the 2007-2008 NPSAS, 15 percent of all students received state financial aid.

[86] This survey is a central repository for information on state support of students and families paying for postsecondary education.

[87] The District of Columbia and Puerto Rico also reported that they use federal methodology.

aid organizations and institutional officials we interviewed.[88] Some schools require students to provide information in addition to the FAFSA, such as filling out the College Board's PROFILE form or submitting tax returns. One official said the PROFILE provides more detailed information on a family's assets, such as home equity and retirement account balances, which helps the university prioritize the students with the most need.

Institutional officials we interviewed said their schools considered savings in 529 plans as assets, even if they used different methodologies to calculate their financial aid or included the assets at different percentages. Officials at two institutions said they did not consider savings in 529 plans beyond how they are already reported by the family on the FAFSA. An official at a third institution said the school does not collect any additional information on savings in 529 plans beyond what is requested on the FAFSA even though the school requires families to fill out the PROFILE form and uses an institutional methodology to award its financial aid. The remaining institutional officials said they collect additional family financial information when calculating student aid, but consider savings in 529 plans similarly to the family's other assets. Specifically, one institutional official said her school uses the PROFILE form to gather more detailed information about a family's financial situation. Even so, 529 plan savings do not affect a student's need any differently than other assets, she said, which are assessed by the institution at about five percent of their value. Additionally, she said 529 plan assets are considered parental assets even if they are reported as student assets because the school assesses parental assets at a lower percentage. An official at another institution said her school assesses assets at around 20 percent of their value when calculating the EFC for institutional aid.

Officials' opinions varied on whether savings in 529 plans should affect financial aid, but many said families' concerns that these savings will have an adverse effect are common. One state financial aid official said it would be helpful if 529 plan savings were excluded entirely from the calculation because including them can be a deterrent to saving. She said her office often encounters families who feel penalized for saving

---

[88] According to the 2007-2008 NPSAS, 22 percent of all students received institutional financial aid.

because they believe the students without savings receive financial aid. Likewise, a 529 plan official said regardless of whether the student's financial aid will be reduced by savings in a 529 plan, there is the perception that it will. In contrast, one institutional financial aid official said savings in 529 plans should not be treated any differently than other assets because the need analysis is meant to determine the family's fair share of college expenses and excluding 529 plans would be counter to this aim. One researcher we interviewed found that the issue may be most important for those families who are on the margin of receiving federal financial aid. Regardless of the perceived effect 529 plan savings may have on financial aid, some of the officials we interviewed said they encourage families to save for college because much of the aid they may be offered could be in the form of loans, so saving will generally be in the student's long-term financial interest.

Concluding Observations

As currently designed, 529 college savings plans benefit a small percentage of U.S. families. In general these families tend to be wealthier than others. It is not clear whether the $1.6 billion in federal tax expenditures that these plans represent strategically targets limited federal resources. Although 529 plans do help some families save for college, families with less income and who are uncertain about whether their children will attend college may have less incentive to invest resources in 529 plans than in other forms of savings. In addition, the tax benefits attractive to a higher-income family do not offer as much benefit to a family with lower tax liability.

Questions about who benefits from this tax expenditure occur in an environment of long-term fiscal challenges and difficult choices about how the federal government allocates limited resources. Reviewing 529 plans in conjunction with the other billions of dollars in federal educational assistance provided through tax expenditures, credits, and deductions could help Congress determine whether this program is meeting its goals. Similar to GAO's prior work on higher-education related tax expenditures, our analysis of 529 college savings plans was not able to address all questions that could inform future policy choices regarding 529 plans. For example, what is the purpose of the federal tax benefits provided through 529 plans? Are the goals and objectives clearly defined and measurable? Who is the target population for 529 plans and does the current structure provide appropriate incentives for that population? How do the 529 plan federal tax benefits interact with other programs, such as federal financial aid and other higher education tax benefits and savings vehicles?

Consideration of these questions could facilitate continued congressional oversight of this tax expenditure.

Agency Comments

We provided a draft of this report to Education, Treasury, and IRS for comment. The agencies provided technical comments that were incorporated, as appropriate.

We are sending copies of this report to the Secretary of Education, Secretary of the Treasury, Commissioner of Internal Revenue, relevant congressional committees, and other interested parties. In addition, the report will be available at no charge on the GAO Web site at http://www.gao.gov. If you or your staff have any questions about this report, please contact me at sagerm@gao.gov or 202-512-6806. Contact points for our Offices of Congressional Relations and Public Affairs may be found on the last page of this report. GAO staff who made key contributions to this report are listed in appendix III.

Sincerely yours,

Michelle Sager, Acting Director
Education, Workforce, and Income Security Issues

Appendix I: Objectives, Scope, and Methodology

Our review examined: (1) the percentage and characteristics of families enrolling in 529 plans, (2) the plan features and other factors that affect participation in 529 plans, and (3) the extent to which savings in 529 plans affect financial aid awards. To answer these research objectives, we analyzed government data; interviewed state 529 plan officials from select states as well as industry representatives and academic experts; reviewed plan documents and analyzed industry data; conducted a literature review; interviewed federal, state, and institutional financial aid officials; and reviewed Department of Education (Education) and Internal Revenue Service (IRS) documents as well as relevant federal laws, regulations and guidance.

We assessed the reliability of the data we used by reviewing documentation, interviewing knowledgeable officials, and conducting electronic testing on relevant data fields. We found the data we reviewed reliable for the purposes of our analyses. We conducted this performance audit from November 2011 to December 2012 in accordance with generally accepted government auditing standards. Those standards require that we plan and perform the audit to obtain sufficient, appropriate evidence to provide a reasonable basis for our findings and conclusions based on our audit objectives. We believe that the evidence obtained provides a reasonable basis for our findings and conclusions based on our audit objectives.

Analysis of Government Data

To determine the percentage and characteristics of families enrolling in 529 plans, we reviewed data from the 2010 Survey of Consumer Finances (SCF); the 2007-2008 National Postsecondary Student Aid Study (NPSAS); and 2007-2010 Statistics of Income (SOI) federal tax data. The 2010 SCF, 2007-2008 NPSAS, and 2010 SOI were the most recent data available at the time of our engagement, so to ensure consistency in reporting we adjusted all dollar amounts from previous years' data to 2010 dollars.

Each of these three data sources (SCF, NPSAS, and SOI) are based on probability samples and estimates are formed using the appropriate estimation weights provided with each survey's data. Because each of these samples follows a probability procedure based on random selections, they represent only one of a large number of samples that could have been drawn. Since each sample could have provided different estimates, we express our confidence in the precision of our particular sample's results as a 95 percent confidence interval (e.g., plus or minus 2.5 percentage points). This is the interval that would contain the actual population value for 95 percent of the samples we could have drawn. Unless otherwise noted, all percentage estimates based on the SCF, NPSAS, and SOI have 95 percent confidence intervals that are within 5 percentage points of the estimate itself, and all numerical estimates other than percentages have 95 percent confidence intervals that are within 5 percent of the estimate itself.

For our analysis of the percentage and characteristics of families who held 529 plans, we relied primarily on restricted data from the 2010 SCF. SCF is a triennial survey sponsored by the Board of Governors of the Federal Reserve System (Federal Reserve) to provide detailed information on the finances of U.S. households. The SCF sample of 6,492 households represented approximately 118 million households in 2010. It collects detailed financial characteristics on an economically dominant single individual or couple (married or living as partners) in a household, which we refer to as a family for the purposes of this report.[1] For our analysis, we aggregated financial information so that, unless otherwise noted, all SCF estimates are for the family rather than the individual survey respondent. We did not restrict our analysis to families with children, in part, because 529 plans can be used for nearly anyone, including one's child, grandchild, niece, nephew, and oneself.[2] However, about 88 percent of families with 529 plans or Coverdell Education Savings Accounts (Coverdells),[3] a similar education savings vehicle, had

---

[1] The unit of analysis for the SCF includes this economically dominant individual (or couple) along with economically interdependent individuals (such as minor children) also living in the household.

[2] Additionally, because of the limited number of families in the SCF sample that had 529 plans or Coverdell Education Savings Accounts, we were unable to produce reliable estimates for subgroups of families with these accounts, such as characteristics by age group or by whether families had children living with them. We were, however, able to generate reliable estimates for all families with 529 plans or Coverdell Education Savings Accounts.

[3] Similar to 529 plans, Coverdell accounts allow families to save for education expenses. Account earnings accumulate tax-deferred and earnings included in withdrawals used to pay for qualified education expenses are not subject to federal tax. Unlike 529 plans, (1) Coverdell contributors must generally have a modified adjusted gross income of less than $110,000 per year ($220,000 in the case of a joint return), (2) Coverdells have annual contribution limits of $2,000 that must generally stop when a beneficiary reaches 18 years of age, and (3) Coverdells can be used for qualified elementary, secondary, or postsecondary expenses typically for individuals under age 30. These Coverdell features will be affected if the changes in the Economic Growth and Tax Relief Reconciliation Act of 2001 are not extended.

children 25 years of age or younger living with them. Our estimates for 529 plans included Coverdells because Federal Reserve officials said respondents did not always distinguish between the two account types; therefore, we did not separate these responses because of data reliability concerns. However, the officials indicated that a larger share of the SCF respondents reported having 529 plans than Coverdells. Further, using SOI data, we estimate that in 2010 approximately 85 percent of tax filers who took a distribution from either a 529 plan or a Coverdell reported distributions from a 529 plan while 14 percent reported distributions from a Coverdell and 1 percent reported distributions from both. We wrote an analysis program that the Federal Reserve ran using their restricted SCF dataset to separate information on Medical Savings Accounts and Health Savings Accounts, which had been included in the 2010 public dataset with 529 plans and Coverdells. Federal Reserve officials modified some resulting information to protect the privacy of survey respondents, for example by rounding dollar amounts.

Using SCF, we generated estimates on the percentage and characteristics of families enrolled in 529 plans or Coverdells and of families not enrolled in these plans. We examined family characteristics such as wealth (financial assets), income, education, and race or ethnicity. To calculate financial assets, we used the methodology the Federal Reserve uses to produce variables for its published Bulletin articles. This methodology included assets held in checking, savings, and brokerage accounts, certificates of deposit, mutual funds, stocks, bonds, life insurance, retirement accounts, and other vehicles such as 529 plans. Assets held in retirement accounts included those in defined contribution plans (e.g. a 401(k), individual retirement account, or thrift savings plan) as well as in traditional pensions or defined benefit plans. To calculate income, we used the family's self-reported total income. To report the family's highest educational attainment, we reviewed the education of each respondent and his or her partner or spouse and included whichever was higher. We reported information on the respondent's race or ethnicity, which does not necessarily indicate the race or ethnicity of other family members.[4]

We used 2007-2008 NPSAS data to develop a similar demographic profile for college students and generate other estimates on college costs

---

[4] Further, the respondent is not necessarily the head of the household.

and financial aid amounts. NPSAS is a comprehensive study by Education that examines how students and their families pay for higher education. It includes nationally representative samples of 113,535 undergraduates, 12,585 graduate students, and 1,581 first-professional students[5] enrolled any time between July 1, 2007 and June 30, 2008. The NPSAS data are based on administrative records and student interviews, and NPSAS includes survey results from both students who received financial aid and those who did not. While we used NPSAS to develop a demographic profile for college students similar to the one we developed for the general population using SCF, families with 529 plans are not directly comparable to families of college students. For example, while our estimates using SCF are for all families (including families with children in college, with children not in college, and with no children), our estimates for families using NPSAS are exclusively for families with a current college student. In NPSAS, families include the student and the student's parents (if the student is dependent) or the student's spouse and dependents (if the student is independent). Further, the population of NPSAS students' families is not the same as the population of families with a child in college because a family may have more than one student in college in a given year. Consequently students' family characteristics derived from NPSAS are not directly comparable to family characteristics based on the SCF, though for the purposes of our report we use similar terminology to describe them. Similar to our analysis of SCF, we generated estimates of the characteristics of college students' families— including income,[6] education, and race or ethnicity. To report income, we calculated the total income of (1) the student's parents (if the student was dependent) and (2) the student and the student's spouse (if the student was independent). To report the family's highest educational attainment, we reviewed the education of each student's mother and father and included whichever was higher. We also reported information on the student's race or ethnicity, which does not necessarily indicate the race or ethnicity of other family members. We also developed separate estimates for students who are considered either dependent on their parents or independent for financial aid purposes.

---

[5] First-professional students are students pursuing degrees in fields such as pharmacy, dentistry, medicine, or law.

[6] Information was not available on the assets for families of college students.

We also used NPSAS to generate other estimates related to the cost of college and amount of financial aid awards. First, we estimated the median annual cost of attendance at 4-year public and private non-profit institutions. This included tuition and fees, room and board, transportation, and personal expenses, though the estimate is valid only for students who attended one institution. Second, we estimated the percentage of students who received grants and loans, as well as the median amount of these grants and loans and the percent and amount of college expenses remaining. Third, we generated estimates for the proportion of students who filled out the Free Application for Federal Student Aid (FAFSA) and, for those who did fill out the FAFSA, the proportion who met certain criteria to have assets excluded from the federal expected family contribution (EFC) and the proportion whose assets affected the EFC. Finally, we calculated the percentage of students who received state and institutional financial aid.

We also analyzed 2007-2010 taxpayer data from SOI to determine the extent to which taxpayers used distributions from 529 plans for qualified education expenses and how the tax savings from these plans were distributed across income levels. The SOI individual tax return file is a stratified probability sample of income returns filed with the IRS. The SOI sample of 308,583 returns represented approximately 143 million tax returns filed for 2010. We combined data from the SOI individual tax file with information from the Form 1099-Q. A 529 plan must file a Form 1099-Q with the IRS and the account owner or beneficiary each time a taxpayer receives a distribution from a 529 plan account.[7] This form includes information on the amount of the distribution and the earnings (or loss) on the distribution. When taxpayers receive a Form 1099-Q, they must determine if the distribution was used for qualified education expenses. If the distribution, or any portion of it, was nonqualified, the earnings portion is subject to taxes and, in some cases, a penalty. The taxpayer determines the amount of taxes and penalty owed on the nonqualified distribution by completing Form 5329, which is contained in the individual tax return file. By combining information from the 1099-Q with information in the individual tax return file, we identified the percentage of taxpayers who reported nonqualified distributions that were

---

[7] Distributions from a 529 plan include those used for qualified education expenses as well as those used for nonqualified expenses or refunds to the account owner or beneficiary.

subject to a penalty.[8] We also used SOI data to estimate the tax savings by using the National Bureau of Economic Research's (NBER) TAXSIM Model, a microsimulation model of U.S. federal and state income tax systems.[9] TAXSIM calculates estimated liabilities under U.S. federal and state income tax laws from actual tax returns that have been prepared for public use by the Statistics of Income Division of the IRS.[10] Our analysis of the tax savings from 529 plans excludes returns with a filing status of married filing separately.

Interviews with State 529 Plan Representatives, Academic Experts, and Industry Representatives

To provide information on the factors that affect participation we interviewed officials from the following five state 529 plans and their industry partners: Louisiana, Michigan, Pennsylvania, Utah, and Virginia. We used College Savings Plan Network (CSPN) data to select states that represented a variety of plan types (direct-sold, advisor-sold, and pre-paid), offered a number of features (i.e., various state tax benefits, state matching program), and were geographically diverse. We also used suggestions provided by academic experts and industry representatives to inform our selection as well as to provide information on 529 plan participation. We interviewed academic researchers (including the Center for Social Development), industry regulators (the Financial Industry Regulatory Authority and the Municipal Securities Rulemaking Board), financial services companies (American Funds and UPromise), financial experts (such as Financial Research Corporation and Morningstar), College Savings Plan Network, Savingforcollege.com, and consumer interest groups (Investment Company Institute and the American Association of Individual Investors).

Analysis of Plan and Industry Data and Documentation

We analyzed CSPN data on state 529 plans to provide a national overview of plan features, such as fees and state tax benefits. Biennially, states submit plan data to CSPN through an online system to be posted

---

[8] While earnings on all distributions are subject to a tax if the distribution was not used for qualified education expenses, the penalty is waived under certain circumstances, such as when a beneficiary dies or receives a scholarship.

[9] NBER provided GAO with a copy of TAXSIM that we executed within our secure tax computing environment.

[10] See Daniel Feenberg and Elisabeth Coutts, "An Introduction to the TAXSIM Model," *Journal of Policy Analysis and Management*, vol. 12, no. 1, (1993): 189-194.

on the CSPN website. CSPN provided us with data on each state as of July 2012. We analyzed the data for every state for both direct-sold and advisor-sold plans on the following features: whether the state offers a matching grant program, whether the state offers tax deductions for contributions and the amount, whether the state offers tax credits for contributions and the amount, types of investment options offered, total contribution limits, and required initial contribution amounts. We also analyzed the following fee categories: program manager fee, state fee, annual account maintenance fee, miscellaneous fee, annual distribution fee, estimated underlying fund expenses, total annual asset-based fees, maximum deferred sales charge, and minimum initial sales charge.

Further, we compared CSPN disclosure principles with direct-sold plan disclosure documentation for the five states we interviewed. We reviewed the extent to which the selected states incorporated elements of the CSPN disclosure principles and whether plan documentation was easily comparable across states. Specifically, we compared whether the state documents contained eleven elements outlined in the principles, including: a summary of key features, an assessment of the individual summary features, a statement of any guarantee by the state issuer or the state, information on state tax treatment and other benefits, information that the state offers more than one plan, fee descriptions, and investment risks, among others. These elements were chosen based on discussions with states and experts who identified plan fees, tax benefits, and investment options as some of the most important features consumers consider when choosing whether or not to participate in a 529 plan. In addition to recording whether states have disclosed the information listed above, we assessed whether any information was missing, where the information was located in the document, and any other observations about the ability to find and understand plan information.

Literature Review

We reviewed studies conducted by academics, researchers, industry representatives, and federal agencies on why families choose to participate in 529 plans and what features might serve as barriers or incentives. We identified literature published since 2006, when Congress passed the Pension Protection Act of 2006, Pub. L. No. 109-250, which made permanent the tax-exemption on 529 plan distributions used for qualified education expenses. Our review included scholarly/peer reviewed material, government reports, hearings and transcripts, trade/industry articles, association/nonprofit/think tank publications, and working papers. We searched information sources such as EconLit,

ProQuest, ERIC, PolicyFile, WorldCat, ECO, PapersFirst, ArticleFirst, and
Academic OneFile. These online sources are nationally recognized
databases that index and abstract research literature. We selected search
terms to capture literature that specifically addressed 529 plans, college
savings plans, qualified state tuition programs, and prepaid tuition. Of the
32 studies we identified, 12 studies met the following criteria: 1) included
information on plan features in specific states, 2) addressed the
consequences for consumers of choosing one type of 529 plan over
another, 3) identified barriers or incentives for consumers to choose 529
plans, 4) included data collected by states on plan participation, and/or, 5)
included information on plan disclosures to consumers. All studies cited in
the report were reviewed by at least two GAO analysts. Studies that
included statistical methods were reviewed by a GAO statistician and
social science analyst. All studies were reviewed for methodological
soundness and to ensure that any limitations associated with study
methodologies were conveyed to readers in our report text, footnotes, or
this appendix.

Financial Aid Analysis

To understand the extent to which savings in 529 plans affect federal
financial aid awards, we interviewed Education officials in the Office of
Postsecondary Education. We also reviewed relevant statutory
provisions, the FAFSA, the Federal Student Aid Handbook, and other
Education documents related to calculating the EFC.

To understand the extent to which savings in 529 plans are considered in
state financial aid calculations, we interviewed officials from state financial
aid offices in six states. To select the state financial aid offices, we used
information from a 2009-2010 survey by the National Association of State
Student Grant and Aid Programs to identify states that indicated they
used a financial aid formula other than the federal methodology in their
primary needs analysis and/or provided special treatment for state 529
plans. For report consistency, we selected the same states selected for
529 plan site visit locations to the extent possible (i.e., where the data
supported the selection based on the criteria). We interviewed
representatives in the following state financial aid offices: Louisiana Office
of Student Financial Assistance, Michigan Office of Scholarships and
Grants, New York Higher Education Services Corporation, Pennsylvania
Higher Education Assistance Agency, Utah Higher Education Assistance
Authority, and State Council of Higher Education for Virginia.

We also selected six institutions from the states whose financial aid
offices were selected for interviews. To obtain a national perspective on

institutional financial aid and determine the best method for selecting the individual institutions, we interviewed representatives at several financial aid organizations including the Association of Private Sector Colleges and Universities, the College Board, the National Association of Student Financial Aid Administrators, the National Association of Independent Colleges and Universities, and the American Association of Community Colleges. In these interviews, some officials said that schools with larger endowments were likely to require families to provide additional information, such as that required on the College Board's PROFILE application, to award their institutional financial aid.[11] We matched the 2012-2013 College Board's list of institutions that use the PROFILE application with Education's 2009-2010 Integrated Postsecondary Education Data System to calculate endowment amounts per student at public and private non-profit four-year institutions. We also reviewed the list of schools that participate in the Private 529 Consortium and selected at least one school that was also part of this group. One state did not have an institution that used the PROFILE application so we reviewed websites of postsecondary schools in that state to identify a school that collected data in addition to the FAFSA. We interviewed representatives at the following institutions: Xavier University of Louisiana, University of Michigan, St. Lawrence University, Swarthmore College, University of Utah, and University of Richmond.

---

[11] The College Board is a not-for-profit membership organization that provides college students with financial aid support and scholarships. It also conducts research and advocacy on behalf of students, educators, schools, and colleges. The PROFILE is an application developed by the College Board to help institutions gather information used to award nonfederal student aid funds.

Appendix II: Free Application for Federal Student Aid, 2012-2013

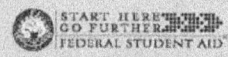

⇒FAFSA℠
U.S. DEPARTMENT OF EDUCATION
FEDERAL STUDENT AID

FREE APPLICATION FOR FEDERAL STUDENT AID
July 1, 2012 — June 30, 2013

START HERE
GO FURTHER
FEDERAL STUDENT AID

Use this form to apply free for federal and state student grants, work-study and loans.

Or apply free online at www.fafsa.gov.

Applying by the Deadlines

For federal aid, submit your application as early as possible, but no earlier than January 1, 2012. We must receive your application no later than June 30, 2013. Your college must have your correct, complete information by your last day of enrollment in the 2012-2013 school year.

For state or college aid, the deadline may be as early as January 2012. See the table to the right for state deadlines. You may also need to complete additional forms.

Check with your high school guidance counselor or a financial aid administrator at your college about state and college sources of student aid and deadlines.

If you are filing close to one of these deadlines, we recommend you file online at **www.fafsa.gov.** This is the fastest and easiest way to apply for aid.

Using Your Tax Return

If you (or your parents) need to file a 2011 income tax return with the Internal Revenue Service (IRS), we recommend that you complete it before filling out the FAFSA. If you have not completed your return yet, you can submit your FAFSA now using estimated tax information, and then correct that information after you file your return.

The easiest way to complete or correct your FAFSA with accurate tax information is by using the IRS Data Retrieval Tool through **www.fafsa.gov.** In a few simple steps, you may be able to view your tax return information and transfer it directly into your FAFSA.

Filling Out the FAFSA℠

If you or your family has unusual circumstances that might affect your financial situation (such as loss of employment), complete this form to the extent you can, then submit it as instructed and consult with the financial aid office at the college you plan to attend.

For help in filling out the FAFSA, go to **www.studentaid.ed.gov/completefafsa** or call 1-800-4-FED-AID (1-800-433-3243). TTY users (for the hearing impaired) may call 1-800-730-8913.

Fill the answer fields directly on your screen or print the form and complete it by hand. Your answers will be read electronically; therefore if you complete the form by hand:

- use black ink and fill in circles completely:
- print clearly in CAPITAL letters and skip a box between words:
- report dollar amounts (such as $12,356.41) like this:

Correct ● Incorrect ⊗ ✓

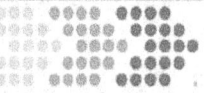

Orange is for student information and purple is for parent information.

Mailing Your FAFSA℠

After you complete this application, make a copy of pages 3 through 8 for your records. Then mail the original of pages 3 through 8 to:

Federal Student Aid Programs, P.O. Box 4692, Mt. Vernon, IL 62864-4692.

After your application is processed, you will receive a summary of your information in your *Student Aid Report* (SAR). If you provide an e-mail address, your SAR will be sent by e-mail within 3-5 days. If you do not provide an e-mail address, your SAR will be mailed to you within three weeks. If you would like to check the status of your FAFSA, go to **www.fafsa.gov** or call 1-800-4-FED-AID.

Let's Get Started!

Now go to page 3 of the application form and begin filling it out. Refer to the notes as instructed.

APPLICATION DEADLINES
Federal Aid Deadline - June 30, 2013
State Aid Deadlines - See below.

Check with your financial aid administrator for these states and territories:

AL, AS *, AZ, CO, FM *, GA, GU *, HI *, MH *, MP *, NE, NM, NV *, PR, PW *, SD *, TX, UT, VA *, VI *, WA, WI and WY *.

Pay attention to the symbols that may be listed after your state deadline.

AK	AK Education Grant and AK Performance Scholarship - June 30, 2012 (date received)
AR	Academic Challenge - June 1, 2012 (date received) Workforce Grant - Contact the financial aid office. Higher Education Opportunity Grant - June 1, 2012 (date received)
CA	Initial awards - March 2, 2012 + * Additional community college awards - September 2, 2012 (date postmarked) + *
CT	February 15, 2012 (date received) # *
DC	June 30, 2012 (date received) * For priority consideration, submit application by May 15, 2012.
DE	April 15, 2012 (date received)
FL	May 15, 2012 (date processed)
IA	July 1, 2012 (date received); earlier priority deadlines may exist for certain programs.
ID	Opportunity Grant - March 1, 2012 (date received) # *
IL	As soon as possible after January 1, 2012. Awards made until funds are depleted.
IN	March 10, 2012 (date received)
KS	April 1, 2012 (date received) # *
KY	As soon as possible after January 1, 2012. Awards made until funds are depleted.
LA	June 30, 2013 (July 1, 2012 recommended)
MA	May 1, 2012 (date received) #
MD	March 1, 2012 (date received)
ME	May 1, 2012 (date received)
MI	March 1, 2012 (date received)
MN	30 days after term starts (date received)
MO	April 2, 2012 (date received)
MS	MTAG and MESG Grants - September 15, 2012 (date received) HELP Scholarship - March 31, 2012 (date received) #
MT	March 1, 2012 (date received) #
NC	As soon as possible after January 1, 2012. Awards made until funds are depleted.
ND	April 15, 2012 (date received) # Early priority deadlines may exist for institutional programs.
NH	NH is not offering a state grant this year.
NJ	2011-2012 Tuition Aid Grant recipients - June 1, 2012 (date received) All other applicants - October 1, 2012, fall & spring terms (date received) - March 1, 2013, spring term only (date received)
NY	June 30, 2013 (date received) + *
OH	October 1, 2012 (date received)
OK	March 1, 2012 (date received) #
OR	OSAC Private Scholarships - March 1, 2012 (date received) Oregon Opportunity Grant - February 1, 2012 (date received)
PA	All first time applicants at a community college; a business/trade/technical school; a hospital school of nursing; or enrolled in a non-transferable two year program - August 1, 2012 (date received) All other applicants - May 1, 2012 (date received)
RI	March 1, 2012 (date received) #
SC	Tuition Grants - June 30, 2012 (date received) SC Commission on Higher Education - As soon as possible after January 1, 2012. Awards made until funds are depleted.
TN	State Grant - As soon as possible after January 1, 2012. Awards made until funds are depleted. State Lottery - September 1, 2012 (date received) #
VT	As soon as possible after January 1, 2012. Awards made until funds are depleted. *
WV	Promise Scholarship - March 1, 2012 (date received) # * WV Higher Education Grant Program - April 16, 2012 (date received) #

For priority consideration, submit application by date specified.
+ Applicants encouraged to obtain proof of mailing.
* Additional form may be required.

Federal Student Aid logo, name (and FAFSA) are registered trademarks of Federal Student Aid, U.S. Department of Education.

STATE AID DEADLINES

Notes for questions 14 and 15 (page 3)

If you are an eligible noncitizen, write in your eight- or nine-digit Alien Registration Number. Generally, you are an eligible noncitizen if you are (1) a permanent U.S. resident with a Permanent Resident Card (I-551); (2) a conditional permanent resident with a Conditional Green Card (I-551C); (3) the holder of an Arrival-Departure Record (I-94) from the Department of Homeland Security showing any one of the following designations: "Refugee," "Asylum Granted," "Parolee" (I-94 confirms that you were paroled for a minimum of one year and status has not expired), T-Visa holder (T-1, T-2, T-3. etc.) or "Cuban-Haitian Entrant;" or (4) the holder of a valid certification or eligibility letter from the Department of Health and Human Services showing a designation of "Victim of human trafficking."

If you are in the U.S. on an F1 or F2 student visa, a J1 or J2 exchange visitor visa, or a G series visa (pertaining to international organizations), select "No. I am not a citizen or eligible noncitizen." You will not be eligible for federal student aid; however, you should still complete the application because you may be eligible for state or college aid.

Notes for questions 16 and 17 (page 3)

Report your marital status as of the date you sign your FAFSA. If your marital status changes after you sign your FAFSA, check with the financial aid office at the college. According to the Defense of Marriage Act (1996), "...the word 'marriage' means a legal union between one man and one woman as husband and wife, and the word 'spouse' refers to a person of the opposite sex who is a husband or a wife." Therefore, same-sex unions are not considered marriages for federal purposes, including the FAFSA.

Notes for question 22 (page 3)

The Selective Service System, and the registration requirement for young men, preserves America's ability to provide manpower in an emergency to the U.S. Armed Forces. Almost all men—ages 18 through 25—must register. For more information about Selective Service, visit www.sss.gov.

Notes for questions 33 (page 4) and 80 (page 6)

If you filed or will file a foreign tax return, a tax return with Puerto Rico, another U.S. territory (e.g., Guam, American Samoa, the U.S. Virgin Islands, Swain's Island or the Northern Marianas Islands) or one of the Freely Associated States (i.e., the Republic of Palau, the Republic of the Marshall Islands or the Federated States of Micronesia), use the information from that return to fill out this form. If you filed a foreign return, convert all monetary units to U.S. dollars, using the exchange rate that is in effect today. To view the daily exchange rate, go to www.federalreserve.gov/releases/h10/current.

Notes for questions 34 (page 4) and 81 (page 6)

In general, a person is eligible to file a 1040A or 1040EZ if he or she makes less than $100,000, does not itemize deductions, does not receive income from his or her own business or farm and does not receive alimony. A person is not eligible to file a 1040A or 1040EZ if he or she makes $100,000 or more, itemizes deductions, receives income from his or her own business or farm, is self-employed, receives alimony or is required to file Schedule D for capital gains. If you filed a 1040 only to claim American Opportunity, Hope or Lifetime Learning credits, and you would have otherwise been eligible for a 1040A or 1040EZ, answer "Yes" to this question. If you filed a 1040 and were not required to file a tax return, answer "Yes" to this question.

Notes for questions 37 (page 4) and 85 (page 7) — Notes for those who filed a 1040EZ

On the 1040EZ, if a person didn't check either box on line 5, enter 01 if he or she is single, or 02 if he or she is married. If a person checked either the "you" or "spouse" box on line 5, use 1040EZ worksheet line F to determine the number of exemptions ($3,700 equals one exemption).

Notes for questions 41 and 42 (page 4) and 89 and 90 (page 7)

Net worth means current value minus debt. If net worth is negative, enter 0.

Investments include real estate (do not include the home you live in), trust funds, UGMA and UTMA accounts, money market funds, mutual funds, certificates of deposit, stocks, stock options, bonds, other securities, installment and land sale contracts (including mortgages held), commodities, etc.

Investments also include qualified educational benefits or education savings accounts (e.g., Coverdell savings accounts, 529 college savings plans and the refund value of 529 prepaid tuition plans). For a student who does not report parental information, the accounts owned by the student (and/or the student's spouse) are reported as student investments in question 41. For a student who must report parental information, the accounts are reported as parental investments in question 89, including all accounts owned by the student and all accounts owned by the parents for any member of the household.

Investments do not include the home you live in, the value of life insurance, retirement plans (401[k] plans, pension funds, annuities, non-education IRAs, Keogh plans, etc.) or cash, savings and checking accounts already reported in questions 40 and 88.

Investments also do not include UGMA and UTMA accounts for which you are the custodian, but not the owner.

Investment value means the current balance or market value of these investments as of today. Investment debt means only those debts that are related to the investments.

Business and/or investment farm value includes the market value of land, buildings, machinery, equipment, inventory, etc. Business and/or investment farm debt means only those debts for which the business or investment farm was used as collateral.

Business value does not include the value of a small business if your family owns and controls more than 50 percent of the business and the business has 100 or fewer full-time or full-time equivalent employees. For small business value, your family includes (1) persons directly related to you, such as a parent, sister or cousin, or (2) persons who are or were related to you by marriage, such as a spouse, stepparent or sister-in-law.

Investment farm value does not include the value of a family farm that you (your spouse and/or your parents) live on and operate.

Notes for questions 48 (page 5)

Answer "Yes" if you are currently serving in the U.S. Armed Forces or are a National Guard or Reserves enlistee who is on active duty for other than state or training purposes.

Answer "No" if you are a National Guard or Reserves enlistee who is on active duty for state or training purposes.

Notes for question 49 (page 5)

Answer "Yes" (you are a veteran) if you (1) have engaged in active duty in the U.S. Armed Forces (Army, Navy, Air Force, Marines or Coast Guard) or are a National Guard or Reserve enlistee who was called to active duty for other than state or training purposes, or were a cadet or midshipman at one of the service academies, and (2) were released under a condition other than dishonorable. Also answer "Yes" if you are not a veteran now but will be one by June 30, 2013.

Answer "No" (you are not a veteran) if you (1) have never engaged in active duty in the U.S. Armed Forces, (2) are currently an ROTC student or a cadet or midshipman at a service academy, (3) are a National Guard or Reserve enlistee activated only for state or training purposes, or (4) were engaged in active duty in the U.S. Armed Forces but released under dishonorable conditions.

Also answer "No" if you are currently serving in the U.S. Armed Forces and will continue to serve through June 30, 2013.

Page 2

Notes continued on page 9.

➤FAFSA™
U.S. DEPARTMENT OF EDUCATION
FEDERAL STUDENT AID

FREE APPLICATION FOR FEDERAL STUDENT AID
July 1, 2012 — June 30, 2013

START HERE
GO FURTHER
FEDERAL STUDENT AID

Step One (Student): For questions 1-31, leave blank any questions that do not apply to you (the student). OMB # 1845-0001

Your full name (**exactly as it appears on your Social Security card**) If your name has a suffix, such as Jr. or III, include a space between your last name and suffix.

1. Last name	2. First name	3. Middle initial

Your mailing address

4. Number and street (include apt. number)

5. City (and country if not U.S.)

6. State

7. ZIP code

8. Your Social Security Number

9. Your date of birth — MONTH DAY YEAR — 1 9

10. Your permanent telephone number ( ) —

Your driver's license number and driver's license state (if you have one)

11. Driver's license number

12. Driver's license state

13. Your e-mail address. If you provide your e-mail address, we will communicate with you electronically. For example, when your FAFSA has been processed, you will be notified by e-mail. Your e-mail address will also be shared with your state and the colleges listed on your FAFSA to allow them to communicate with you. If you prefer to be contacted by postal mail or do not have an e-mail address, leave this field blank.

@

14. Are you a U.S. citizen? Mark only one. See Notes page 2.
- Yes, I am a U.S. citizen (U.S. national). **Skip to question 16.** ○ 1
- No, but I am an eligible noncitizen. **Fill in question 15.** ○ 2
- No, I am not a citizen or eligible noncitizen. **Skip to question 16.** ○ 3

15. Alien Registration Number
A

16. What is your marital status as of today? See Notes page 2.
- I am single ○ 1
- I am married/remarried ○ 2
- I am separated ○ 3
- I am divorced or widowed ○ 4

17. Month and year you were married, remarried, separated, divorced or widowed. See Notes page 2.
MONTH YEAR

18. What is your state of legal residence?
STATE

19. Did you become a legal resident of this state before January 1, 2007?
- Yes ○ 1
- No ○ 2

20. If the answer to question 19 is "No," give month and year you became a legal resident.
MONTH YEAR

21. Are you male or female?
- Male ○ 1
- Female ○ 2

22. **If female, skip to question 23.** Most male students must register with Selective Service to receive federal aid. If you are male, age 18-25 and not registered, fill in the circle and we will register you. See Notes page 2.
- Register me ○ 1

23. Have you been convicted for the possession or sale of illegal drugs for an offense that occurred while you were receiving federal student aid (such as grants, loans or work-study)?
Answer "No" if you have never received federal student aid or if you have never had a drug conviction while receiving federal student aid. If you have a drug conviction for an offense that occurred while you were receiving federal student aid, answer "Yes," but complete and submit this application, and we will mail you a worksheet to help you determine if your conviction affects your eligibility for aid. If you are unsure how to answer this question, call 1-800-433-3243 for help.
- No ○ 1
- Yes ○ 2

Some states and colleges offer aid based on the level of schooling your parents completed.

24. Highest school your father completed — Middle school/Jr. high ○ 1 — High school ○ 2 — College or beyond ○ 3 — Other/unknown ○ 4

25. Highest school your mother completed — Middle school/Jr. high ○ 1 — High school ○ 2 — College or beyond ○ 3 — Other/unknown ○ 4

26. When you begin college in the 2012-2013 school year, what will be your high school completion status?
- High school diploma. **Answer question 27.** ○ 1
- General Educational Development (GED) certificate. **Skip to question 28.** ○ 2
- Homeschooled. **Skip to question 28.** ○ 3
- None of the above. **Skip to question 28.** ○ 4

For Help — www.studentaid.ed.gov/completefafsa — Page 3 — Step One CONTINUED on page 4

Step One CONTINUED from page 3

27. What is the name of the high school where you received or will receive your high school diploma? Enter the complete high school name, and the city and state where the high school is located.

High School Name

High School City

STATE

28. Will you have your first bachelor's degree before July 1, 2012?

Yes ○ ¹   No ○ ²

29. When you begin the 2012-2013 school year, what will be your grade level?

Never attended college and 1st year undergraduate .... ○ ⁰

Attended college before and 1st year undergraduate .... ○ ¹

2nd year undergraduate/sophomore .... ○ ²

3rd year undergraduate/junior .... ○ ³

4th year undergraduate/senior .... ○ ⁴

5th year/other undergraduate................................. ○ ⁵

1st year graduate/professional .... ○ ⁶

Continuing graduate/professional or beyond..................... ○ ⁷

30. When you begin the 2012-2013 school year, what degree or certificate will you be working on?

1st bachelor's degree .... ○ ¹

2nd bachelor's degree .... ○ ²

Associate degree (occupational or technical program) .... ○ ³

Associate degree (general education or transfer program)......... ○ ⁴

Certificate or diploma (occupational, technical or education program of less than two years)...................................... ○ ⁵

Certificate or diploma (occupational, technical or education program of two or more years) .... ○ ⁶

Teaching credential (nondegree program)...................... ○ ⁷

Graduate or professional degree .... ○ ⁸

Other/undecided .... ○ ⁹

31. Are you interested in being considered for work-study?

Yes ○ ¹   No ○ ²   Don't know ○ ³

Step Two (Student): Answer questions 32–57 about yourself (the student). If you are single, separated, divorced or widowed, answer only about yourself. If you are married or remarried as of today, include information about your spouse (husband or wife).

32. For 2011, have you (the student) completed your IRS income tax return or another tax return listed in question 33?

I have already completed my return .... ○ ¹

I will file but have not yet completed my return .... ○ ²

I'm not going to file. **Skip to question 38.** .... ○ ³

33. What income tax return did you file or will you file for 2011?

IRS 1040 .... ○ ¹

IRS 1040A or 1040EZ .... ○ ²

A foreign tax return. **See Notes page 2.** .... ○ ³

A tax return with Puerto Rico, another U.S. territory, or Freely Associated State. **See Notes page 2.** .... ○ ⁴

34. If you have filed or will file a 1040, were you eligible to file a 1040A or 1040EZ? **See Notes page 2.**

Yes ○ ¹   No ○ ²   Don't know ○ ³

For questions 35–44, if the answer is zero or the question does not apply to you, enter 0. Report whole dollar amounts with no cents.

35. What was your (and spouse's) adjusted gross income for 2011? Adjusted gross income is on IRS Form 1040—line 37; 1040A—line 21; or 1040EZ—line 4.

$ ☐☐☐,☐☐☐

36. Enter your (and spouse's) income tax for 2011. Income tax amount is on IRS Form 1040—line 55; 1040A—line 35; or 1040EZ—line 10.

$ ☐☐☐,☐☐☐

37. Enter your (and spouse's) exemptions for 2011. Exemptions are on IRS Form 1040—line 6d or Form 1040A—line 6d. For Form 1040EZ, **see Notes page 2.**

☐☐

Questions 38 and 39 ask about earnings (wages, salaries, tips, etc.) in 2011. Answer the questions whether or not a tax return was filed. This information may be on the W-2 forms, or on IRS Form 1040—lines 7 + 12 + 18 + Box 14 (Code A) of IRS Schedule K-1 (Form 1065); on 1040A—line 7; or on 1040EZ—line 1. If any individual earning item is negative, do not include that item in your calculation.

38. How much did you earn from working in 2011?

$ ☐☐☐,☐☐☐

39. How much did your spouse earn from working in 2011?

$ ☐☐☐,☐☐☐

40. As of today, what is your (and spouse's) total current balance of cash, savings and checking accounts? **Don't include** student financial aid.

$ ☐☐☐,☐☐☐

41. As of today, what is the net worth of your (and spouse's) investments, including real estate? **Don't include** the home you live in. Net worth means current value minus debt. **See Notes page 2.**

$ ☐☐☐,☐☐☐

42. As of today, what is the net worth of your (and spouse's) current businesses and/or investment farms? **Don't include** a family farm or family business with 100 or fewer full-time or full-time equivalent employees. **See Notes page 2.**

$ ☐☐☐,☐☐☐

Step Two CONTINUED from page 4

43. Student's 2011 Additional Financial Information (Enter the combined amounts for you and your spouse.)

a. Education credits (American Opportunity, Hope or Lifetime Learning tax credits) from IRS Form 1040—line 49 or 1040A—line 31. $ [ ][ ][ ][ ][ ]

b. Child support paid because of divorce or separation or as a result of a legal requirement. **Don't include** support for children in your household, as reported in question 93. $ [ ][ ][ ][ ][ ]

c. Taxable earnings from need-based employment programs, such as Federal Work-Study and need-based employment portions of fellowships and assistantships. $ [ ][ ][ ][ ][ ]

d. Taxable student grant and scholarship aid **reported to the IRS in your adjusted gross income**. Includes AmeriCorps benefits (awards, living allowances and interest accrual payments), as well as grant and scholarship portions of fellowships and assistantships. $ [ ][ ][ ][ ][ ]

e. Combat pay or special combat pay. Only enter the amount that was taxable and included in your adjusted gross income. **Don't include** untaxed combat pay. $ [ ][ ][ ][ ][ ]

f. Earnings from work under a cooperative education program offered by a college. $ [ ][ ][ ][ ][ ]

44. Student's 2011 Untaxed Income (Enter the combined amounts for you and your spouse.)

a. Payments to tax-deferred pension and savings plans (paid directly or withheld from earnings), including, but not limited to, amounts reported on the W-2 forms in Boxes 12a through 12d, codes D, E, F, G, H and S. $ [ ][ ][ ][ ][ ]

b. IRA deductions and payments to self-employed SEP, SIMPLE, Keogh and other qualified plans from IRS Form 1040—line 28 + line 32 or 1040A—line 17. $ [ ][ ][ ][ ][ ]

c. Child support received for any of your children. **Don't include** foster care or adoption payments. $ [ ][ ][ ][ ][ ]

d. Tax exempt interest income from IRS Form 1040—line 8b or 1040A—line 8b. $ [ ][ ][ ][ ][ ]

e. Untaxed portions of IRA distributions from IRS Form 1040—lines (15a minus 15b) or 1040A—lines (11a minus 11b). Exclude rollovers. If negative, enter a zero here. $ [ ][ ][ ][ ][ ]

f. Untaxed portions of pensions from IRS Form 1040—lines (16a minus 16b) or 1040A—lines (12a minus 12b). Exclude rollovers. If negative, enter a zero here. $ [ ][ ][ ][ ][ ]

g. Housing, food and other living allowances paid to members of the military, clergy and others (including cash payments and cash value of benefits). **Don't include** the value of on-base military housing or the value of a basic military allowance for housing. $ [ ][ ][ ][ ][ ]

h. Veterans noneducation benefits, such as Disability, Death Pension, or Dependency & Indemnity Compensation (DIC) and/or VA Educational Work Study allowances. $ [ ][ ][ ][ ][ ]

i. Other untaxed income not reported in items 44a through 44h, such as workers' compensation, disability, etc. Also include the first-time homebuyer tax credit from IRS Form 1040—line 67. **Don't include** student aid, earned income credit, additional child tax credit, welfare payments, untaxed Social Security benefits, Supplemental Security Income, Workforce Investment Act educational benefits, on-base military housing or a military housing allowance, combat pay, benefits from flexible spending arrangements (e.g., cafeteria plans), foreign income exclusion or credit for federal tax on special fuels. $ [ ][ ][ ][ ][ ]

j. Money received, or paid on your behalf (e.g., bills), not reported elsewhere on this form. $ [ ][ ][ ][ ][ ]

Step Three (Student): Answer the questions in this step to determine if you will need to provide parental information. Once you answer "Yes" to any of the questions in this step, skip Step Four and go to Step Five on page 8.

45. Were you born before January 1, 1989? ....   Yes ○   No ○

46. As of today, are you married? (Also answer "Yes" if you are separated but not divorced.) ....   Yes ○   No ○

47. At the beginning of the 2012-2013 school year, will you be working on a master's or doctorate program (such as an MA, MBA, MD, JD, PhD, EdD, graduate certificate, etc.)? ....   Yes ○   No ○

48. Are you currently serving on active duty in the U.S. Armed Forces for purposes other than training? See Notes page 2 .   Yes ○   No ○

49. Are you a veteran of the U.S. Armed Forces? See Notes page 2 ....   Yes ○   No ○

50. Do you have children who will receive more than half of their support from you between July 1, 2012 and June 30, 2013? .   Yes ○   No ○

51. Do you have dependents (other than your children or spouse) who live with you and who receive more than half of their support from you, now and through June 30, 2013? ....   Yes ○   No ○

52. At any time since you turned age 13, were both your parents deceased, were you in foster care or were you a dependent or ward of the court? See Notes page 9 . ...   Yes ○   No ○

53. As determined by a court in your state of legal residence, are you or were you an emancipated minor? See Notes page 9 . ....   Yes ○   No ○

54. As determined by a court in your state of legal residence, are you or were you in legal guardianship? See Notes page 9 . .....   Yes ○   No ○

55. At any time on or after July 1, 2011, did your high school or school district homeless liaison determine that you were an unaccompanied youth who was homeless? See Notes page 9 . ...   Yes ○   No ○

56. At any time on or after July 1, 2011, did the director of an emergency shelter or transitional housing program funded by the U.S. Department of Housing and Urban Development determine that you were an unaccompanied youth who was homeless? See Notes page 9 . ...   Yes ○   No ○

57. At any time on or after July 1, 2011, did the director of a runaway or homeless youth basic center or transitional living program determine that you were an unaccompanied youth who was homeless or were self-supporting and at risk of being homeless? See Notes page 9 . ...   Yes ○   No ○

For Help — www.studentaid.ed.gov/completefafsa   Page 5

If you (the student) answered "No" to every question in Step Three, go to Step Four.
If you answered "Yes" to any question in Step Three, skip Step Four and go to Step Five on page 8.
(Health professions students: Your college may require you to complete Step Four even if you answered "Yes" to any Step Three question.)
If you believe that you are unable to provide parental information, see Notes page 9.

Step Four (Parent): Complete this step if you (the student) answered "No" to all questions in Step Three.

Answer all the questions in Step Four even if you do not live with your parents. Grandparents, foster parents, legal guardians, aunts and uncles are not considered parents on this form unless they have legally adopted you. If your parents are living and married to each other, answer the questions about them. If your parent is single, widowed, divorced, separated or remarried, see the Notes on page 9 for additional instructions.

58. What is your parents' marital status as of today?

Married or remarried ...... ○ 1   Divorced or separated .... ○ 3

Single .... ○ 2   Widowed .... ○ 4

59. Month and year they were married, remarried, separated, divorced or widowed.   MONTH   YEAR

What are the Social Security Numbers, names and dates of birth of the parents reporting information on this form?
If your parent does not have a Social Security Number, you must enter 000-00-0000. If the name includes a suffix, such as Jr. or III, include a space between the last name and suffix. Enter two digits for each day and month (e.g., for May 31, enter 05 31).

60. FATHER'S/STEPFATHER'S SOCIAL SECURITY NUMBER   **61.** FATHER'S/STEPFATHER'S LAST NAME, AND   **62.** FIRST INITIAL   **63.** FATHER'S/STEPFATHER'S DATE OF BIRTH   1 9

64. MOTHER'S/STEPMOTHER'S SOCIAL SECURITY NUMBER   **65.** MOTHER'S/STEPMOTHER'S LAST NAME, AND   **66.** FIRST INITIAL   **67.** MOTHER'S/STEPMOTHER'S DATE OF BIRTH   1 9

68. Your parents' e-mail address. If you provide your parents' e-mail address, we will let them know your FAFSA has been processed. This e-mail address will also be shared with your state and the colleges listed on your FAFSA to allow them to electronically communicate with your parents.

@

69. What is your parents' state of legal residence?   STATE

70. Did your parents become legal residents of this state before January 1, 2007?   Yes ○ 1   No ○ 2

71. If the answer to question 70 is "No," give the month and year legal residency began for the parent who has lived in the state the longest.   MONTH   YEAR

72. How many people are in your parents' household?
Include:
- yourself, even if you don't live with your parents;
- your parents;
- your parents' other children if (a) your parents will provide more than half of their support between July 1, 2012 and June 30, 2013, or (b) the children could answer "No" to every question in Step Three; and
- other people if they now live with your parents, your parents provide more than half of their support and your parents will continue to provide more than half of their support between July 1, 2012 and June 30, 2013.

73. How many people in your parents' household (from question 72) will be college students between July 1, 2012 and June 30, 2013? Always count yourself as a college student. Do not include your parents. You may include others only if they will attend, at least half-time in 2012-2013, a program that leads to a college degree or certificate.

In 2010 or 2011, did you, your parents or anyone in your parents' household (from question 72) receive benefits from any of the federal programs listed? Mark all that apply. Answering these questions will not reduce eligibility for student aid or these programs. Supplemental Nutrition Assistance Program (SNAP) is the new name for Food Stamps. SNAP, Food Stamps and/or TANF may have a different name in your parents' state. Call 1-800-4-FED-AID to find out the name of the state's program.

74. Supplemental Security Income (SSI) ○   **75. Food Stamps** ○   **76. Free or Reduced Price Lunch** ○   **77. Temporary Assistance for Needy Families (TANF)** ○   **78. Special Supplemental Nutrition Program for Women, Infants and Children (WIC)** ○

79. For 2011, have your parents completed their IRS income tax return or another tax return listed in question 80?

My parents have already completed their return. .... ○ 1

My parents will file but have not yet completed their return. .... ○ 2

My parents are not going to file. **Skip to question 86.** .... ○ 3

80. What income tax return did your parents file or will they file for 2011?

IRS 1040 .... ○ 1

IRS 1040A or 1040EZ .... ○ 2

A foreign tax return. **See Notes page 2.** .... ○ 3

A tax return with Puerto Rico, another U.S. territory or Freely Associated State. **See Notes page 2.** .... ○ 4

81. If your parents have filed or will file a 1040, were they eligible to file a 1040A or 1040EZ? See Notes page 2.   Yes ○ 1   No ○ 2   Don't know ○ 3

82. As of today, is either of your parents a dislocated worker? See Notes page 9.   Yes ○ 1   No ○ 2   Don't know ○ 3

For Help — 1-800-433-3243   Page 6   Step Four CONTINUED on page 7

Step Four CONTINUED from page 6

For questions 83–92, if the answer is zero or the question does not apply, enter 0. Report whole dollar amounts with no cents.

83. What was your parents' adjusted gross income for 2011? Adjusted gross income is on IRS Form 1040—line 37; 1040A—line 21; or 1040EZ—line 4.

84. Enter your parents' income tax for 2011. Income tax amount is on IRS Form 1040—line 55; 1040A—line 35; or 1040EZ—line 10.

85. Enter your parents' exemptions for 2011. Exemptions are on IRS Form 1040—line 6d or on Form 1040A—line 6d. For Form 1040EZ, see Notes page 2.

Questions 86 and 87 ask about earnings (wages, salaries, tips, etc.) in 2011. Answer the questions whether or not a tax return was filed. This information may be on the W-2 forms, or on IRS Form 1040—lines 7 + 12 + 18 + Box 14 (Code A) of IRS Schedule K-1 (Form 1065); on 1040A—line 7; or on 1040EZ—line 1. If any individual earning item is negative, do not include that item in your calculation.

86. How much did your father/stepfather earn from working in 2011?

87. How much did your mother/stepmother earn from working in 2011?

88. As of today, what is your parents' total current balance of cash, savings and checking accounts?

89. As of today, what is the net worth of your parents' investments, including real estate? **Don't include** the home in which your parents live. Net worth means current value minus debt. See Notes page 2.

90. As of today, what is the net worth of your parents' current businesses and/or investment farms? **Don't include** a family farm or family business with 100 or fewer full-time or full-time equivalent employees. See Notes page 2.

91. Parents' 2011 Additional Financial Information (Enter the amounts for your parent(s).)

   a. Education credits (American Opportunity, Hope or Lifetime Learning tax credits) from IRS Form 1040—line 49 or 1040A—line 31.

   b. Child support paid because of divorce or separation or as a result of a legal requirement. **Don't include** support for children in your parents' household, as reported in question 72.

   c. Your parents' taxable earnings from need-based employment programs, such as Federal Work-Study and need-based employment portions of fellowships and assistantships.

   d. Your parents' taxable student grant and scholarship aid **reported to the IRS in your parents' adjusted gross income.** Includes AmeriCorps benefits (awards, living allowances and interest accrual payments), as well as grant and scholarship portions of fellowships and assistantships.

   e. Combat pay or special combat pay. Only enter the amount that was taxable and included in your parents' adjusted gross income. Do not enter untaxed combat pay.

   f. Earnings from work under a cooperative education program offered by a college.

92. Parents' 2011 Untaxed Income (Enter the amounts for your parent(s).)

   a. Payments to tax-deferred pension and savings plans (paid directly or withheld from earnings), including, but not limited to, amounts reported on the W-2 forms in Boxes 12a through 12d, codes D, E, F, G, H and S.

   b. IRA deductions and payments to self-employed SEP, SIMPLE, Keogh and other qualified plans from IRS Form 1040—line 28 + line 32 or 1040A—line 17.

   c. Child support received for any of your parents children. **Don't include** foster care or adoption payments.

   d. Tax exempt interest income from IRS Form 1040—line 8b or 1040A—line 8b.

   e. Untaxed portions of IRA distributions from IRS Form 1040—lines (15a minus 15b) or 1040A—lines (11a minus 11b). Exclude rollovers. If negative, enter a zero here.

   f. Untaxed portions of pensions from IRS Form 1040—lines (16a minus 16b) or 1040A—lines (12a minus 12b). Exclude rollovers. If negative, enter a zero here.

   g. Housing, food and other living allowances paid to members of the military, clergy and others (including cash payments and cash value of benefits). **Don't include** the value of on-base military housing or the value of a basic military allowance for housing.

   h. Veterans noneducation benefits, such as Disability, Death Pension, or Dependency & Indemnity Compensation (DIC) and/or VA Educational Work-Study allowances.

   i. Other untaxed income not reported in items 92a through 92h, such as workers' compensation, disability, etc. Also include the first-time homebuyer tax credit from IRS Form 1040—line 67. **Don't include** student aid, earned income credit, additional child tax credit, welfare payments, untaxed Social Security benefits, Supplemental Security Income, Workforce Investment Act educational benefits, on-base military housing or a military housing allowance, combat pay, benefits from flexible spending arrangements (e.g. cafeteria plans), foreign income exclusion or credit for federal tax on special fuels.

Step Five (Student): Complete this step only if you (the student) answered "Yes" to any questions in Step Three.

93. How many people are in your household?
Include:
- yourself (and your spouse),
- your children, if you will provide more than half of their support between July 1, 2012 and June 30, 2013, and
- other people if they now live with you, you provide more than half of their support and you will continue to provide more than half of their support between July 1, 2012 and June 30, 2013.

94. How many people in your (and your spouse's) household (from question 93) will be college students between July 1, 2012 and June 30, 2013? Always count yourself as a college student. Include others only if they will attend, at least half time in 2012-2013, a program that leads to a college degree or certificate.

In 2010 or 2011, did you (or your spouse) or anyone in your household (from question 93) receive benefits from any of the federal programs listed? Mark all that apply. Answering these questions will not reduce eligibility for student aid or these programs. Supplemental Nutrition Assistance Program (SNAP) is the new name for Food Stamps. SNAP, Food Stamps and/or TANF may have a different name in your state. Call 1-800-4-FED-AID to find out the name of the state's program.

| 95. Supplemental Security Income (SSI) ○ | 96. Food Stamps ○ | 97. Free or Reduced Price Lunch ○ | 98. Temporary Assistance for Needy Families (TANF) ○ | 99. Special Supplemental Nutrition Program for Women, Infants and Children (WIC) ○ |

100. As of today, are you (or your spouse) a dislocated worker? See Notes page 9.   Yes ○   No ○   Don't know ○

Step Six (Student): Indicate which colleges you want to receive your FAFSA information.

Enter the six-digit federal school code and your housing plans. You can find the school codes at **www.fafsa.gov** or by calling 1-800-4-FED-AID. If you cannot get the code, write in the complete name, address, city and state of the college. For state aid, you may wish to list your preferred college first. To find out how to have more colleges receive your FAFSA information, read **What is the FAFSA?** on page 10.

HOUSING PLANS

101.a 1st FEDERAL SCHOOL CODE   OR NAME OF COLLEGE / ADDRESS AND CITY   STATE   101.b on campus ○ / with parent ○ / off campus ○

101.c 2ND FEDERAL SCHOOL CODE   OR NAME OF COLLEGE / ADDRESS AND CITY   STATE   101.d on campus ○ / with parent ○ / off campus ○

101.e 3RD FEDERAL SCHOOL CODE   OR NAME OF COLLEGE / ADDRESS AND CITY   STATE   101.f on campus ○ / with parent ○ / off campus ○

101.g 4TH FEDERAL SCHOOL CODE   OR NAME OF COLLEGE / ADDRESS AND CITY   STATE   101.h on campus ○ / with parent ○ / off campus ○

Step Seven (Student and Parent): Read, sign and date.

If you are the student, by signing this application you certify that you (1) will use federal and/or state student financial aid only to pay the cost of attending an institution of higher education, (2) are not in default on a federal student loan or have made satisfactory arrangements to repay it, (3) do not owe money back on a federal student grant or have made satisfactory arrangements to repay it, (4) will notify your college if you default on a federal student loan and (5) will not receive a Federal Pell Grant from more than one college for the same period of time.

If you are the parent or the student, by signing this application you agree, if asked, to provide information that will verify the accuracy of your completed form. This information may include U.S. or state income tax forms that you filed or are required to file. Also, you certify that you understand that **the Secretary of Education has the authority to verify information reported on this application with the Internal Revenue Service and other federal agencies.** If you sign any document related to the federal student aid programs electronically using a personal identification number (PIN), you certify that you are the person identified by the PIN and have not disclosed that PIN to anyone else. If you purposely give false or misleading information, you may be fined up to $20,000, sent to prison, or both.

102. Date this form was completed
MONTH   DAY   2012 ○   or   2013 ○

103. Student (Sign below)

Parent (A parent from Step Four sign below.)

If you or your family paid a fee for someone to fill out this form or to advise you on how to fill it out, that person must complete this part.

Preparer's name, firm and address

104. Preparer's Social Security Number (or 105)

105. Employer ID number (or 104)

106. Preparer's signature and date

COLLEGE USE ONLY   FEDERAL SCHOOL CODE

D/O ○   Homeless Youth Determination ○

FAA Signature

DATA ENTRY USE ONLY: ○ P   ○ *   ○ L   ○ E

For Help — 1-800-433-3243   Page 8

Notes for question 52 (page 5)

Answer "**Yes**" if at any time since you turned age 13:

- You had no living parent (biological or adoptive), even if you are now adopted; or
- You were in foster care, even if you are no longer in foster care today; or
- You were a dependent or ward of the court, even if you are no longer a dependent or ward of the court today. For federal student aid purposes, someone who is incarcerated is not considered a ward of the court.

The financial aid administrator at your school may require you to provide proof that you were in foster care or a dependent or ward of the court.

Notes for questions 53 and 54 (page 5)

The definition of legal guardianship does not include your parents, even if they were appointed by a court to be your guardians. You are also not considered a legal guardian of yourself.

Answer "**Yes**" if you can provide a copy of a court's decision that as of today you are an emancipated minor or are in legal guardianship. Also answer "**Yes**" if you can provide a copy of a court's decision that you were an emancipated minor or were in legal guardianship immediately before you reached the age of being an adult in your state. The court must be located in your state of legal residence at the time the court's decision was issued.

Answer "**No**" if you are still a minor and the court decision is no longer in effect or the court decision was not in effect at the time you became an adult.

The financial aid administrator at your college may require you to provide proof that you were an emancipated minor or in legal guardianship.

Notes for questions 55–57 (page 5)

Answer "**Yes**" if you received a determination at any time on or after July 1, 2011, that you were an unaccompanied youth who was homeless or, for question 57, at risk of being homeless.

- "**Homeless**" means lacking fixed, regular and adequate housing. You may be homeless if you are living in shelters, parks, motels or cars, or are temporarily living with other people because you have nowhere else to go. Also, if you are living in any of these situations and fleeing an abusive parent you may be considered homeless even if your parent would provide support and a place to live.
- "**Unaccompanied**" means you are not living in the physical custody of your parent or guardian.
- "**Youth**" means you are 21 years of age or younger or you are still enrolled in high school as of the day you sign this application.

Answer "**No**" if you are not homeless or at risk of being homeless, or do not have a determination. You should contact your financial aid office for assistance if you do not have a determination but believe you are an unaccompanied youth who is homeless or are an unaccompanied youth providing for your own living expenses who is at risk of being homeless.

The financial aid administrator at your college may require you to provide a copy of the determination if you answered "**Yes**" to any of these questions.

Notes for students unable to provide parental information on pages 6 and 7

Under very limited circumstances (for example, your parents are incarcerated; you have left home due to an abusive family environment; or you do not know where your parents are and are unable to contact them), you may be able to submit your FAFSA without parental information. **If you are unable to provide parental information**, skip Steps Four and Five, and go to Step Six. Once you submit your FAFSA without parental data, **you must follow up with the financial aid office at the college you plan to attend**, in order to complete your FAFSA.

Notes for Step Four, questions 58–92 (pages 6 and 7)

Additional instructions about who is considered a parent on this form:

- If your parent is widowed or single, answer the questions about that parent.
- If your widowed parent is remarried as of today, answer the questions about that parent and your stepparent.
- If your parents are divorced or separated, answer the questions about the parent you lived with more during the past 12 months. (If you did not live with one parent more than the other, give answers about the parent who provided more financial support during the past 12 months, or during the most recent year that you actually received support from a parent.) If this parent is remarried as of today, answer the questions about that parent and your stepparent.

Notes for questions 82 (page 6) and 100 (page 8)

In general, a person may be considered a dislocated worker if he or she:

- is receiving unemployment benefits due to being laid off or losing a job and is unlikely to return to a previous occupation;
- has been laid off or received a lay-off notice from a job;
- was self-employed but is now unemployed due to economic conditions or natural disaster; or
- is a displaced homemaker. A displaced homemaker is generally a person who previously provided unpaid services to the family (e.g., a stay-at-home mom or dad), is no longer supported by the husband or wife, is unemployed or underemployed, and is having trouble finding or upgrading employment.

If a person quits work, generally he or she is not considered a dislocated worker even if, for example, the person is receiving unemployment benefits.

Answer "**Yes**" to question 82 if your parent is a dislocated worker. Answer "**Yes**" to question 100 if you or your spouse is a dislocated worker.

Answer "**No**" to question 82 if your parent is not a dislocated worker. Answer "**No**" to question 100 if neither you nor your spouse is a dislocated worker.

Answer "**Don't know**" to question 82 if you are not sure whether your parent is a dislocated worker. Answer "**Don't know**" to question 100 if you are not sure whether you or your spouse is a dislocated worker. You can contact your financial aid office for assistance in answering these questions.

The financial aid administrator at your college may require you to provide proof that your parent is a dislocated worker, if you answered "**Yes**" to question 82, or that you or your spouse is a dislocated worker, if you answered "**Yes**" to question 100.

Page 9

What is the FAFSA™?

Why fill out a FAFSA?

The *Free Application for Federal Student Aid* (FAFSA) is the first step in the financial aid process. You use the FAFSA to apply for federal student aid, such as grants, loans and work-study. In addition, most states and colleges use information from the FAFSA to award nonfederal aid.

Why all the questions?

The questions on the FAFSA are required to calculate your Expected Family Contribution (EFC). The EFC measures your family's financial strength and is used to determine your eligibility for federal student aid. Your state and the colleges you list may also use some of your responses. They will determine if you may be eligible for school or state aid, in addition to federal aid.

How do I find out what my Expected Family Contribution (EFC) is?

Your EFC will be listed on your *Student Aid Report* (SAR). Your SAR summarizes the information you submitted on your FAFSA. It is important to review your SAR to make sure all of your information is correct and complete. Make corrections or provide additional information, as necessary.

How much aid will I receive?

Using the information on your FAFSA and your EFC, the financial aid office at your college will determine the amount of aid you will receive. The college will use your EFC to prepare a financial aid package to help you meet your financial need. Financial need is the difference between your EFC and your college's cost of attendance (which can include living expenses), as determined by the college. If you or your family have unusual circumstances that should be taken into account, contact your college's financial aid office. Some examples of unusual circumstances are: unusual medical or dental expenses or a large change in income from last year to this year.

When will I receive the aid?

Any financial aid you are eligible to receive will be paid to you through your college. Typically, your college will first use the aid to pay tuition, fees and room and board (if provided by the college). Any remaining aid is paid to you for your other educational expenses. If you are eligible for a Federal Pell Grant, you may receive it from only one college for the same period of enrollment.

How can I have more colleges receive my FAFSA information?

If you are completing a paper FAFSA, you can only list four colleges in the school code step. You may add more colleges by doing one of the following:

1. Use the Federal Student Aid PIN you will receive after your FAFSA has been processed and go to *FAFSA on the Web* at **www.fafsa.gov**. Click the "Start Here" button to log in and then select the "Make FAFSA Corrections" link.

2. Use the *Student Aid Report* (SAR), which you will receive after your FAFSA is processed. Your Data Release Number (DRN) verifies your identity and will be listed on the first page of your SAR. You can call 1-800-4-FED-AID and provide your DRN to a customer service representative, who will add more school codes for you.

3. Provide your DRN to the financial aid administrator at the college you want added, and he or she can add their school code to your FAFSA.

Note: Your FAFSA record can only list up to ten school codes. If there are ten school codes on your record, any new school codes that you add will replace one or more of the school codes listed.

Where can I receive more information on student aid?

The best place for information about student financial aid is the financial aid office at the college you plan to attend. The financial aid administrator can tell you about student aid available from your state, the college itself and other sources.

- You can also visit our web site **www.studentaid.ed.gov**.
- For information by phone you can call our Federal Student Aid Information Center at 1-800-4-FED-AID (1-800-433-3243). TTY users (for the hearing impaired) may call 1-800-730-8913.
- You can also check with your high school counselor, your state aid agency or your local library's reference section.

Information about other nonfederal assistance may be available from foundations, religious organizations, community organizations and civic groups, as well as organizations related to your field of interest, such as the American Medical Association or American Bar Association. Check with your parents' employers or unions to see if they award scholarships or have tuition payment plans.

Information on the Privacy Act and use of your Social Security Number

We use the information that you provide on this form to determine if you are eligible to receive federal student financial aid and the amount that you are eligible to receive. Sections 483 and 484 of the Higher Education Act of 1965, as amended, give us the authority to ask you and your parents these questions, and to collect the Social Security Numbers of you and your parents. We use your Social Security Number to verify your identity and retrieve your records, and we may request your Social Security Number again for those purposes.

State and institutional student financial aid programs may also use the information that you provide on this form to determine if you are eligible to receive state and institutional aid and the need that you have for such aid. Therefore, we will disclose the information that you provide on this form to each institution you list in questions 101a - 101h, state agencies in your state of legal residence and the state agencies of the states in which the colleges that you list in questions 101a - 101h are located.

If you are applying solely for federal aid, you must answer all of the following questions that apply to you: 1-9, 14-16, 18, 21-23, 26, 28-29, 32-36, 38-58, 60-67, 69, 72-84, 86-100, 102-103. If you do not answer these questions, you will not receive federal aid.

Without your consent, we may disclose information that you provide to entities under a published "routine use." Under such a routine use, we may disclose information to third parties that we have authorized to assist us in administering the above programs; to other federal agencies under computer matching programs, such as those with the Internal Revenue Service, Social Security Administration, Selective Service System, Department of Homeland Security, Department of Justice and Veterans Affairs; to your parents or spouse; and to members of Congress if you ask them to help you with student aid questions.

If the federal government, the U.S. Department of Education, or an employee of the U.S. Department of Education is involved in litigation, we may send information to the Department of Justice, or a court or adjudicative body, if the disclosure is related to financial aid and certain conditions are met. In addition, we may send your information to a foreign, federal, state, or local enforcement agency if the information that you submitted indicates a violation or potential violation of law, for which that agency has jurisdiction for investigation or prosecution. Finally, we may send information regarding a claim that is determined to be valid and overdue to a consumer reporting agency. This information includes identifiers from the record; the amount, status and history of the claim; and the program under which the claim arose.

State Certification

By submitting this application, you are giving your state financial aid agency permission to verify any statement on this form and to obtain income tax information for all persons required to report income on this form.

The Paperwork Reduction Act of 1995

The Paperwork Reduction Act of 1995 says that no one is required to respond to a collection of information unless it displays a valid OMB control number, which for this form is 1845-0001. The time required to complete this form is estimated to be three hours, including time to review instructions, search data resources, gather the data needed, and complete and review the information collection. If you have comments about this estimate or suggestions for improving this form, please write to:

U.S. Department of Education, Washington, DC 20202-4700.

We may request additional information from you to process your application more efficiently. We will collect this additional information only as needed and on a voluntary basis.

Page 10

Appendix III: GAO Contacts and Staff Acknowledgments

GAO Contacts	Michelle Sager, Acting Director, Education, Workforce, and Income Security Issues, 202-512-6806 or sagerm@gao.gov.
Staff Acknowledgments	In addition to the contact named above, Gretta Goodwin (Assistant Director), Amy Anderson, Rachel Beers, and Laura Henry contributed to all aspects of this report. Also making key contributions were Carl Barden, James Bennett, Nora Boretti, Jessica Botsford, Jason Bromberg, Alicia Cackley, Melinda Cordero, Patrick Dudley, Shannon Finnegan, Kim Frankena, Mark Glickman, David Lewis, Ashley McCall, John Mingus, Mark Ramage, MaryLynn Sergent, George Scott, Walter Vance, Kathleen van Gelder, and Michelle Loutoo Wilson.